Living
THROUGH
TROUBLED TIMES

Valerie ~
I pray that this
book blessed you!
♡ Dianne Sellers

Valerie ~

Thank you

please

book please

read!

♡ Emma

Living THROUGH TROUBLED TIMES

Witnessing the Rainbow

A 21-Day Inspirational Journey

DIANNE TOLLIVER

Xulon Press
2301 Lucien Way #415
Maitland, FL 32751
407.339.4217
www.XulonPress.com

Unless otherwise indicated, Scripture quotations taken from the Holy
Bible, New International Version (NIV). Copyright © 1973, 1978, 1984,
2011 by Biblica, Inc.™. Used by permission. All rights reserved.

Scripture quotations taken from the King James Version
(KJV) – *public domain.*

Prayer of St. Francis de Sales – *public domain*

Printed in the United States of America

ISBN-13: 978-1-54560-735-0

Dedication

To Mom, Scott, Bev, and Nan...
Thank you for supporting me
during the storms of life -
while God carried me.

Thank you to all the amazing people who bravely
and openly shared their inspirational stories
to make this book a reality.

A Special Note
of Appreciation and Thanks

The following people provided outstanding support
during the book review process. I will forever be grateful.

Barbara Butler
Bunni Cooper
Jonny Coleman
Bev Hayes
Barbara Heard

Contents

Foreword

It was extremely cloudy, and the storms were forming once again. I had finished the last meeting for my company before my official corporate layoff was in effect. I felt a bit numb as I traveled through the mountains reflecting on the day and the challenges that lay ahead. I knew God was leading me to write this book. I was also keenly aware my layoff came at this particular time, so I would finally and completely trust God with my life. However, I still had doubts. How would I pay the bills? I was worried once again.

As I came over another hill and gazed into the valley, I caught my first glance of the most unbelievable rainbow. It was perfectly nestled in the valley below as if God painted it across the highway right in front of my path. It was unlike any rainbow I had ever seen – it took my breath away. The multi-colored bands were thick, vibrant, and rich. I immediately pulled to the side of the road and knew this is what God had in mind for the cover of my book. I took a few pictures and then continued on my journey in the rain...or so I thought.

As I traveled down the highway, the rainbow intensified and became larger than life. All of a sudden, right under the rainbow, the traffic ahead of me stopped. As I quickly braked, I glanced in my rearview mirror. A black truck going 70 mph was not stopping. I was in trouble. Within a split second, I pulled my small car to the right side of the road to get out of the way. Then, in slow motion, the truck driver slammed on his brakes as his vehicle began to fishtail. At that moment, a silver Jeep slammed into the truck, and they both started to spin out of control. As I glanced out my left window, I realized the Jeep was airborne and spiraling directly toward me. Suddenly, it struck the side of my car and came to rest several yards ahead of me. I was stunned.

Over the next hour, the severity and reality of the situation became clear. The truck and Jeep sustained significant damage, yet no one was injured. Amazingly, only my side mirror was hit by the Jeep; there was no other damage to the car. It simply did not make sense. The mirror was pushed back against the car, metal was showing, and the silver casing around my mirror was gone. There were no other dents, scrapes, or scratches.

Soon, the police arrived. After assessing the accident scene and completing interviews, a police officer stopped to talk with me once again. He clearly stated that moving my car in that split second spared me from severe injury. However, the officer could not understand or explain how the Jeep only hit my mirror, leaving the rest of my car untouched. Adding to the miraculous situation, the momentum from the impact should have pushed my car over the nearby cliff and down the hill. It was as if my car was in a protective bubble; there was simply no logical or scientific explanation.

As the officer examined my mirror, he carefully moved it back to its normal position. Then I noticed the glass of the mirror was untouched, and the mirror control buttons still functioned. As the officer turned his attention to the other drivers, I slowly walked around my car one more time in disbelief. Then, I saw the mirror's silver casing lying on the road. As I slowly bent over to pick it up, I was surprised to discover it was still in one piece with no broken parts. It only had one superficial scratch. The casing fit perfectly over the mirror, and my car required no repairs.

To state the facts—I was spared from severe injury, not once, but twice. Within seconds, from every possible angle while sitting in my car, danger threatened. However, God protected me from harm's way through His unconditional loving grace. I was given a second chance to embrace God's powerful presence, and His never-ending love for me...for all of us.

I now understand. Like you, God has a purpose for my life. I am choosing to trust God completely. He has my full attention. I am writing this book.

> *"He will cover you with his feathers, and under his wings you will find refuge; his faithfulness will be your shield and rampart." Psalm 91:4 (NIV)*

LIVING THROUGH TROUBLED TIMES

Witnessing the Rainbow

Introduction

Life is a journey! Storms will come, and storms will go, but through it all...God is with us!

Growing up in a small town in the middle of the Mojave Desert, I was keenly aware of storms...windstorms. Windstorms would come, and they would go, they were simply a fact of life! Some were a minor nuisance resulting in blown tousled hair, while others literally took my breath away.

Like windstorms, life's personal storms come in all shapes, sizes, forms, and durations. Storms may come in the form of a lost job, work conflicts, betrayal, abuse, money challenges, depression, failures, addictions, illness, and yes - even death. The good news, despite the shape or magnitude of our problems, God is with us! He will carry us through the challenges and obstacles Satan puts in our way as we journey through our lives.

The true stories captured in the pages ahead reflect inspirational journeys my family and friends faced during their personal storms. Due to the sensitive topics discussed, some of the names in the stories were changed. Every chapter concludes with thought-provoking questions to encourage a time for personal reflection and potential next steps you may want to explore.

God cares about ALL our storms, no matter how big or how small they may be. We need to remember to reach out and hold on to His hand and promises as He carries us through our life! We do not need to face our challenges alone. God will carry us through.

May our Heavenly Father speak to your heart as you turn the pages of this book and explore the inspirational journeys of ordinary people who trusted the Lord through their storms.

A New Heart

"Peace I leave with you; my peace I give you. I do not give to you as the world gives. Do not let your hearts be troubled and do not be afraid." John 14:27 (NIV)

It was 4 AM. Suddenly a voice said, "Paul, Paul—wake up! They have a heart for you." "What did you say?" Paul asked as he awoke from a deep sleep. The nurse repeated, "They have a heart for you! It's going to be twelve to twenty-four hours before your surgery, but you're getting a heart!"

Paul, one of fifteen children, grew up in the outskirts of Philadelphia. Growing up in a loving, but poor family, he quickly learned to embrace and value the simple things in life. As an adult, he developed into a caring, vivacious man who embraced his family and all the great things life had to offer. Everyone loved Paul and enjoyed the positive energy he brought to every situation.

Paul's "new heart journey" began with the discovery of a hereditary heart defect that could lead to his death. Due to the rare and unique aspects of his condition, leading surgeons around the country began to study him and his family. Paul, along with his brothers, sisters, and numerous cousins were monitored carefully by many specialists. Life was going great, and Paul's heart was beating strong.

About ten years before Paul's actual transplant, he began to experience some heart irregularities. The doctors decided to insert a heart defibrillator into his upper chest. The implant surgery was a success, and he was expected to make a full recovery. He remained in the hospital overnight so the doctors could monitor him. That evening, Paul and his wife enjoyed a nice visit in his hospital room. Suddenly, with no prior notice, he experienced a feeling that life was draining out of his body. "I'm dying – get the doctor," Paul said. Within thirty seconds, he flat lined.

At that moment, God intervened and took control of Paul's situation. As the doctors frantically worked to bring him back to life, Paul experienced a dramatic intervention that changed his life forever. He could feel God's perfect and comprehensive presence. God was in complete communication with him. "It was amazing–as if I was immersed in total love. I was in a calm sea of peacefulness. I now know first-hand how wonderful His love can be." From that point forward, Paul was never afraid of what faced him during his journey.

The years went by, and he continued to enjoy his career and family. Paul, an eternal optimist, embraced life and looked for ways to be in the Lord's service to others on a daily basis. His goal was to "give back" and focus on "God's will" here on earth. His daily philosophy was to mirror the keywords in the Lord's Prayer:

> *"Our Father which art in heaven, Hallowed be thy name.*
> *Thy kingdom come, Thy will be done on earth,*
> *as it is in heaven." Matthew 6:9-10 (KJV)*

In May of 2013, Paul retired from a successful career where he positively touched hundreds of lives through Christian love. It was now time for him to enjoy the simpler pleasures of life. His heart was doing great. In fact, he was walking six to ten miles a day. However, God had another journey in store for Paul that would allow him to share God's love with hundreds of people once again.

That same summer, Paul's heart took a sudden and dramatic turn for the worse. The muscles of his heart were rapidly thickening and no longer able to efficiently pump blood throughout his body. By September, his doctors broke the news that his heart was failing fast. He needed a heart transplant, and his name was placed on the transplant list.

As Paul began to reach out and notify his family and friends, a remarkable phenomenon began to unfold. He remembered his near-death experience ten years earlier and God's comprehensive love. Throughout the entire search for a heart and leading up to his heart transplant surgery, Paul had complete peace and total serenity at all times – he was never afraid. He had total faith in our all-loving God and knew his life would not have a bad ending. Paul had two wonderful options:

Option 1: He would die and be with Jesus.

Option 2: He would get a new heart and enjoy his family and friends for another twenty years.

Paul had a win/win situation. He openly shared his faith and situation with anyone who was willing to listen. "I'm in God's hands, and those are pretty big hands. I believe in the power of prayer. God will do the right thing for me. I can't lose." Despite Paul's unwavering faith, his family was petrified at the thought of losing their devoted husband, father, brother and friend. He lifted his family up in prayer on a daily basis and released them to God. He trusted God to take care of his family as he turned his attention to the biggest challenge of his life. As always, God was faithful and embraced his entire family as Paul's story unfolded.

Time continued to tick away. By November, his health was drastically deteriorating. Hundreds of people were praying for him across all denominations. Despite his condition, he continued to witness and share his win/win story. Paul reflected, "From my view, I was watching a miracle unfold in slow motion. If you believe in God, then have faith."

In late December, the doctors proactively tried to keep Paul alive while they diligently searched for a heart. On December 19th, they performed an unplanned procedure so he could be home with his family for Christmas. Paul was hospitalized on December 26th as his situation was perilous. He was now in the final stages of heart failure and sleeping twenty-three hours a day. However, he was still sharing his win/win story with any doctor, nurse, pastor, or patient who would listen.

With only days left to live, amazing and emotional news came on a fateful, cold January morning. They found a heart! Later that day, a nurse came rushing into his room and woke Paul up to see a helicopter land only 200 yards away from his hospital room. Through his window, he watched a doctor get off the aircraft carrying a small container which resembled a portable ice chest. The nurse said, "That's Your Heart!" Paul was instantly filled with joy as he watched the doctor disappear into the hospital. The nurse was shocked when Paul jumped out of bed and onto the gurney due to an adrenaline rush. He recalls saying, "Let's go." And with that, they headed to the operating room.

Three years have now passed since Paul's successful heart transplant. Every day, he strives to lead a Godly life and to honor the person who unselfishly donated their heart. He fully embraces the fact someone had to die so he could live. He uses that fact as a positive motivator in his life. Paul thanks and praises God daily for his new heart. He believes his heart donor is watching and holding him accountable to do good things with "their" heart.

Paul's doctors are still amazed and somewhat astonished when they reflect on his positive and incredible transplant journey. In fact, surgeons regularly ask him to sit down and talk with future heart transplant patients who are struggling and sometimes paralyzed with fear. When he looks in the eyes of the patients, he always starts the conversations with a straightforward statement, "If you believe in heaven, you can't lose!" Praise God!

Paul After His Heart Transplant

REFLECTION

1. Are you fully and completely trusting God with your life?
   Yes / Maybe / No

   If you answered maybe or no, what is stopping you from trusting God?

   _____

   _____

   _____

   _____

   _____

   _____

2. Are there some areas in your life where you need to trust God versus trying to control or handle the situation(s) yourself? What are they?

   - _____
   - _____
   - _____
   - _____
   - _____

3. Are you afraid of something or some area in your life?
   Yes / No

   If you answered yes, take a moment and list your fears below.

   I am afraid of _____

   _____

   _____

   _____

I worry that _____

_____

_____

_____

I fear that _____

_____

_____

_____

NEXT STEPS

Take a deep breath. Now, slowly read <u>each</u> fear that you listed in Step 3 above. As you read each fear, add the phrase:

"Lord, please help me to no longer be afraid. I turn this fear over to you. Thank you. Amen."

CLOSING PRAYER

Dear God,

Thank you for unconditionally loving me. Please help me to trust you with all areas of my life. Help me to turn my fears over to you as I look to you for guidance and strength. Thank you for caring about me. You are amazing! Amen.

Losing a Job

"For I know the plans I have for you...plans to prosper
you and not to harm you, plans to give you hope
and a future." Jeremiah 29:11 (NIV)

The cupboards were almost bare. Canned vegetables, beans, and rice were now her primary source of nutrition—the luxury of meat was no longer an option. Bunni had five dollars left in her purse, and the gas company was threatening to turn off her heat. The electricity was recently restored, thanks to the Salvation Army. Despite it all, she was grateful to have a roof over her head and clothes to wear. The months of unemployment were taking their toll. The economy was continuing on a downward slope, and there was no end in sight. What was she going to do?

For over twenty-two years, Bunni enjoyed a successful career working for an international organization in Washington D.C. As a professional software trainer, she taught thousands of people in the United States as well as Saudi Arabia, India, and Indonesia. She was passionate about her job and enjoyed interacting with her students and coworkers. Then one day, without warning, the organization announced the outsourcing of training and technical support as part of a cost savings initiative. Bunni was devastated when she received her layoff notice, and she immediately began to pray for guidance. Fortunately, after many prayers, the organization reconsidered and delayed her layoff for a short period. This delay allowed her to qualify for an early retirement and a reduced pension – a pension that would eventually save her home from foreclosure by the bank.

Two weeks after her layoff, Bunni was hired as an independent training consultant. Life was great for the next four years until the economy encountered a severe recession and companies tightened their belts. The recession resulted in her second layoff. However this time, there was no clear path going forward. She boldly prayed to God for guidance, but there was silence. Despite the silence, she knew God was with her. There was a reason for this challenge in her life, and she kept trusting God. She realized He would help her in His time, not hers.

Due to the weak economy, full-time, part-time, and consulting jobs were nearly impossible to find. As the months of unemployment went on, Bunni expanded her job search to include a Temp Agency where she agreed to accept any work they could offer. She continued to ask God for help and guidance, but very little work came her way. Bunni was thankful for a $300 monthly unemployment check, but that also stopped as she entered her second year without a job. Despite it all, she remained steadfast in her faith and love for God; she knew He had a plan for her life. She garnered considerable comfort from the following Bible verse:

Isaiah 43:1-3 (NIV)

...Do not fear, for I have redeemed you; I have summoned you by name; you are mine. When you pass through the waters, I will be with you; and when you pass through the rivers, they will not sweep over you. When you walk through the fire, you will not be burned; the flames will not set you ablaze. For I am the Lord your God.

Bunni's financial situation was deteriorating quickly, and her life savings were nearly depleted. It was hard to afford gas for the car and food was sparse. Her situation was emotionally draining.

She began renting a bedroom in her home to generate income. It was at this point, Bunni realized her small pension that God blessed her with nearly seven years earlier was keeping the bank from foreclosing on her house. In addition, her home was now providing much-needed income thanks to the spare bedroom. She was grateful.

Then, the warning and shut-off notices started to show up in the mail. At first, the electricity was shut off, but thankfully the Salvation Army stepped in and paid the bill. She received a notification the gas would be turned off at the end of the month, despite her partial monthly payments. Bunni was in serious trouble. Her family and friends had no idea about the hardships she was enduring. She did not want to burden them with her challenges. When she finally let her guard down and shared a glimpse of her financial situation with a few family members, they started to pray. On her darkest days when she did not have the energy to ask God for guidance, she would sing "Jesus Loves Me," a simple but powerful song she learned as a child. It comforted her.

JESUS LOVES ME

Jesus loves me, this I know,
For the Bible tells me so;
Little ones to Him belong;
They are weak, but He is strong

Yes, Jesus loves me!
Yes, Jesus loves me!
Yes, Jesus loves me!
The Bible tells me so.

Lyrics by Anna Bartlett Warner (1827-1915)

Chorus by William Batchelder Bradbury (1816-1868)

As she kept trusting God, Bunni did everything she could think of to fix her situation. Then, something changed. When she called the gas company to inquire about a special "catch-up program" for unemployed people, a dear woman named Mrs. Brown answered her call. It was as if God answered the phone that day. Mrs. Brown went into action and connected Bunni with a Christian Ministries Group who immediately met with her, reviewed her financial situation, and promptly handled the outstanding gas bill. The kind people then shared some upsetting news, "Bunni, you could be considered destitute due to your financial situation. We need to make an appointment for you to come to the food pantry today. You qualify for two grocery bags every time you come because you are below the poverty level." She was devastated as she heard the words and did her best to fight back her tears. She didn't feel destitute. She was thankful to have a roof over her head along with some canned vegetables and rice to eat.

At first, Bunni refused the food pantry offer, but they would not allow her to leave empty handed. After much discussion, she reluctantly found herself sitting in the pantry's lobby waiting for her name to be called. Bunni was disheartened as she slowly glanced around the waiting area and looked into the eyes of the people around her. She had deep empathy for the discouraged, homeless families sitting with her and it hurt her heart. In fact, she felt guilty accepting the food, as she believed the families needed the nourishment much more than she did.

When they finally called her name, she was paralyzed in place and afraid of what she would see on the other side of the wall. A caring lady offered to escort her into the pantry, then softly said, "Pick one item of what you need and fill your bags." Bunni was extremely upset. She had to rely on the lady to help fill her bags with cereal, soup, bread, bananas, and miscellaneous canned goods. She did not accept any meat; she wanted the families to have it. The food helped tremendously, but Bunni never went back. In retrospect, she praised God for the opportunity to experience what it feels like to be dependent on the kindness and generosity of others via the food pantry.

A few weeks later, a small white envelope was discovered partially tucked under Bunni's front doormat. As she examined the envelope and slowly opened it, she screamed and burst into tears. Inside was a life changing gift of $400 all in twenty dollar bills with no note or name. She knew God had her in the palm of His hand and He was on the move! She could feel her joy re-emerging. She faithfully tithed ten percent on her $400. In her words, "When we are faithful by giving our tithes and offerings, God will be faithful to us. We can never out give God."

She finally confided in her pastor and shared the critical financial situation she was facing as well as the miracles that were happening. When another mysterious money gift appeared, Bunni's pastor asked if she would share her story with the church on Sunday morning. She was very hesitant; she did not want people to know about her journey. However, her pastor emphasized that her steadfast faith in God, despite her situation, would allow the church to see "God in action" through other people. It would encourage those who were currently facing personal storms and emphasize the importance of kindness and generosity to others.

After many prayers, Bunni agreed to tell her story which had a significant impact on many people in the church that day. Additional anonymous gifts continued to "show up," and she felt blessed. Soon after that, Bunni received a full-time job she enjoyed for six years before being laid off once again. When the layoff notice came, she did not worry, and she was not afraid. She realized God was in control of her life and He would take care of her.

Today, Bunni is teaching special needs children at an elementary school near her home. Her heart is full of love and gratitude as she enjoys the privilege of working with children who face learning challenges. Bunni endured three years of hardship, but there are key lessons from her story:

- God has a plan for all us, but the adversary places obstacles and hardships in our way to keep us from fulfilling God's purpose for our lives. No matter what happens, we need to keep trusting God! He will make lemonade out of the lemons Satan throws our way.

- We will face storms and trials during our lives. The good news, God will carry us through life's obstacles while He provides us with insights and experiences that prepare us for the next steps in our lives.

- It is important for us to share our stories and how God carries us through our challenges. Our stories provide hope and expose people to God's unconditional love.

- God hears all our prayers. Some prayers are answered immediately, some in God's time (not ours), and some are not answered because God has a different and better plan for us.

- God gives us the gift of community to help us through the tough times in our lives. Reach out and ask for support from your friends and family when you hit life's challenges. Donate to your local food banks and support outreach efforts. If God impresses on your heart to give to the poor or those in need, then follow-through. We are all on this journey together.

Remember, no matter what trials, hardships, heartbreaks, or disappointments you face, God is ALWAYS with you, and He will carry you through life's storms! Simply reach out, and ask Him for help and guidance. Praise God!

Bunni

REFLECTION

1. You never know the journey or challenges someone else is experiencing. Whether it be a stranger, co-worker, friend, or family member, we need to keep our eyes and hearts open to help others in need. The Bible states, "Carry each other's burdens, and in this way, you will fulfill the law of Christ." Galatians 6:2 (NIV)

   a. Pause and Reflect. Have you recently helped someone who is struggling with an area in their life? Have you helped someone today or this week? How have you helped?

   _____

   _____

   _____

   _____

   _____

   b. Do you know a family member, friend, neighbor, or co-worker who needs some help or encouragement? Take a moment and write down their name(s) and how you can help.

NAME	HOW CAN I HELP?	DATE
_____	_____	_____
_____	_____	_____
_____	_____	_____
_____	_____	_____
_____	_____	_____

NEXT STEPS

1. Are you willing to help or encourage at least one of the people you listed above in the next seven days? If you answered yes, add a date when you will provide help or support.

2. Are you struggling with an area or areas in your life where you need help or encouragement? If yes, write down the things that come into your mind:

_____

_____

_____

_____

_____

3. Are you willing to share the challenges you are currently going through with at least one person? If yes, who will you share your challenges with in the next seven days?

_____

_____

_____

_____

CLOSING PRAYER

Have you asked God to help you with the areas you listed above? He is available to listen to you "24 hours a day / 7 days a week (24/7)". Pray this simple prayer:

Dear God,

Thank you for being a loving God who cares about me. I need help with _____. I can no longer do this alone. I am turning my struggles and worries over to you. Please provide me with the wisdom and guidance to overcome my challenges. Help me to trust you going forward. Thank you. Amen.

A Journey to Accept Autism

"As a mother comforts her child, so will I comfort you..."
Isaiah 66:13 (NIV)

Ruby was extremely concerned. Something was unique about her sweet baby boy. She sensed it soon after delivery due to his extreme sensitivity to noise. As the months passed, baby Jon started missing key developmental milestones. At first, babbling, social smiles, and talking were delayed. As Jon continued to slip further and further behind, their daycare provider cautiously raised some concerns. After months of reading and research, despite resistance from her pediatrician and denial from her husband, Ruby pushed for a formal developmental assessment. At thirty-three months, he was diagnosed with a pervasive development disorder on the spectrum of autism complicated by attention deficit hyperactivity disorder (ADHD). Their journey with Jon was just beginning.

Ruby and Franklin's story began several years earlier while attending college. They enjoyed a friendship that blossomed into love. They soon married and settled into their new lives. Ruby's career quickly took off as she began climbing the corporate ladder, while Franklin pursued a fulfilling career in communications. They were an amazing Christian couple full of life, optimism, and love for the Lord.

After five years of marriage and a difficult pregnancy, God blessed them with a beautiful baby girl named Natalie, the apple of their eyes! She was an easy baby and quickly exceeded developmental milestones. Self-driven from an early age, she was reading sight words by age three and reading phonetically before kindergarten. She was a gifted child. Their hopes and dreams for Natalie were endless.

After four years had passed, Ruby received exciting news once again. She was pregnant. As joy and anticipation surrounded this new baby, her husband Franklin became excited at the possibility of a first son and grandson to assume the family name. It was a big deal and particularly important to Franklin since he spent a significant amount of his childhood in foster care. For years, he yearned to have a son and be the type of father he longed for during his childhood.

The day finally came to discover if they were having a boy or girl. When the ultrasound was complete, Ruby's heart pounded with excitement as the technician wrote down their baby's sex on a piece of paper, then quickly slipped it into a sealed envelope. She was full of hopes and dreams for their new baby as she sat down with Franklin that evening and they slowly opened the envelope. They were having a boy!

The next several months were filled with anticipation. Ruby had an easy pregnancy until some anxious moments when her water broke three weeks early. She was rushed into an emergency C-section when baby Jon went into distress due to the umbilical cord wrapping around his neck. Fortunately, things appeared to be fine as Jon's cries filled the delivery room right after he was born. Then, for some reason, the doctor paused and asked, "Did you drink a lot of coffee during your pregnancy?" Through the cloud of C-Section medication, Ruby felt put-off as she immediately sensed concern based on the doctor's question. Was the doctor implying something was wrong with her baby?

As Ruby and Franklin held Jon for the first time, their hearts overflowed with love. He was a beautiful precious baby. Within hours of his delivery, however, Ruby began to notice Jon was extremely jumpy as if he had a hyper-sensitive, nervous response to noise. It was hard to describe but very apparent. Before she left the hospital, she quietly realized there were indicators they would be on a different journey with Jon.

> *"Call to me and I will answer you and tell you*
> *great and unsearchable things you do not know."*
> *Jeremiah 33:3 (NIV)*

For the next three months, Ruby was overwhelmed with Jon's inability to relax. He cried for hours at a time. The confinement of his car seat would leave him screaming. Ruby rarely had relief, but the doctor passed it off as colic and told her it would pass. It was as if this new baby became the new boss and took over their lives. At one point after Jon's non-stop crying, their little girl Natalie said, "Mommy, can we send him back?"

Months passed as the family tried to "settle in" with Jon, but a nagging feeling disturbed Ruby. Something was not right. He remained on target for his physical developmental milestones, but she began to notice some delays in his social, emotional, and communication abilities. At first, she observed his lack of babbling, smiles, and saying simple words. Ruby started to read about child developmental milestones and potential problems that sometimes arise. As his mom, she desperately wanted to help Jon. She longed for him to be successful in life and achieve the dreams she had for him.

As her reading and research progressed, she began to suspect Jon might have a speech or language delay. At his one year appointment, their pediatrician dismissed Ruby's concerns and encouraged her to stop worrying and relax. All of his physical milestones continued to be on target. During this same time, her optimistic husband Franklin tried to reassure Ruby that their little boy was perfect and to stop fretting, but her gut feeling told her something was amiss. She began to feel the weight of Jon's future laid solely on her shoulders and wondered where God was as she desperately tried to help her baby.

When Jon was fourteen months, their day-care provider pulled Ruby aside and raised some concerns. They had noticed differences in Jon compared to his same-age peers. After hearing this, Ruby became obsessed with reading and researching about potential issues and solutions. She needed to "fix" Jon. As Ruby intensified the focus on her baby, Franklin slipped into a state of denial.

At eighteen months, it was evident something was different. Jon was unable to say words and remained in constant motion. He required 100% of Ruby's attention to keep him safe. He would scream when constrained in a high chair or baby swing. Everything he touched went into his mouth including small objects that could be choking hazards. He seemed to use his mouth as a way to interact with things around him. Ruby became frantic regarding the next steps she should take.

As the months progressed, Ruby thought Jon might have ADHD in addition to a speech delay. When she tried to address her concerns with Franklin, he dismissed her suspicions. He had blinders on when it came to his son. Ruby tried to handle the situation by herself, despite her exhausted state. She continued to pray and ask God for help, but her prayers started to feel superficial. Where was God? She needed help.

At Jon's two-year check-up, Ruby felt like an octopus as she tried to hold her son in one place just long enough to express her concerns to the pediatrician regarding Jon's social, emotional, and communication delays. The doctor advised her to wait and see how things progressed in the upcoming year. He did not hear her concerns.

When Ruby left the doctor's office, she was incredibly frustrated and disheartened. Realizing that something must change, she scheduled a follow-up appointment without Jon. During this meeting, Ruby openly shared her list of observations based on her reading and research. She thought Jon might have sensory processing challenges. She also believed some of his behaviors mirrored autism. This time, the pediatrician heard Ruby's plea for help, and he apologized for not listening earlier. She requested names of specialists to have a full developmental assessment conducted. The doctor agreed.

It took nearly six months to obtain an appointment with a child development specialist and an additional three months before Jon's assessment was complete. When the doctor shared the diagnosis, Ruby's fears became a reality. He had a pervasive developmental disorder on the spectrum of autism in addition to ADHD. Franklin was stunned.

Jon's complex and life-altering disability overwhelmed and impacted the entire family. Ruby was determined to resolve his issues so he could live a normal life. Franklin, on the other hand, buried his emotions in his work and pushed forward, while their eight-year-old daughter Natalie started to resent Jon for consuming so much of her parent's time. The challenging situation became the elephant in the room that was uncomfortable to discuss as they each dealt with the devastating news differently. Ruby slowly slipped into a state of depression while Natalie began to feel isolated and alone. Despite his denial, Franklin recognized Jon and his family needed God and a miracle. He began to ask God to heal Jon and help his family on this unplanned journey.

Soon after the assessment, their day-care provider asked them to seek alternative childcare options as they were no longer equipped to handle Jon and his special needs. The necessity to make a change broke Ruby's heart and only intensified the pressure the family was already feeling. After a great deal of research, she contacted Child Find, which was associated with the public schools and their early childhood special education services. A representative from the Child Find team conducted an independent screening and evaluation of Jon. Just before his third birthday, they accepted him into the special needs preschool program. It was during this time he finally said "Mom" for the first time. To supplement preschool, they hired specialized after school care to work with Jon in their home. Ruby continued to invest in therapy toys and books in her quest to correct his challenges.

During this same period, Franklin accepted a new job about an hour from their home. His new role was extremely demanding and required extended hours. Ruby found herself working full time, taking care of their daughter, and carrying the load of Jon's disability. She was exhausted as she plodded through uncharted territory. Ruby did not know where to turn for help or how to accept support from family and friends; the tension between Ruby and Franklin began to build. She could not feel God's support or direction as she tried to control the situation on her own according to the world's rules.

> *"Come to me, all you who are weary and burdened,*
> *and I will give you rest." Matthew 11:28 (NIV)*

As a direct result of the situation, Ruby embarked on a different journey with God. One she never expected to encounter. She was a Christian, believed in the grace of God, and the power of prayer. She also built her life on the principle that if a person does the right things, while carefully following the Ten Commandments and making wise choices, life will yield positive results. Ruby had closely followed "the rules" her entire life, so she was perplexed. Why did God allow this to happen to her innocent child? What caused this? What had she done wrong? She was not angry with God, but extremely confused.

Ruby shared, "I felt as if a hand grenade was thrown into the middle of my life and the basic principles I counted on were turned upside down." There were times when Ruby became disillusioned and disappointed with God as she strived to accept Jon's fate and control the situation on her own. She privately navigated her beliefs and circumstances by burying herself in activities to control her unplanned life.

"He has shown you, O mortal, what is good.
And what does the Lord require of you?
To act justly and to love mercy
and to walk humbly with your God."
Micah 6:8 (NIV)

Some days, Ruby was overwhelmed with sadness as she tried to let go of her dreams for Jon. As she began to accept the reality that her original hopes and expectations would never materialize, she grieved. Birthday parties were especially hard when she saw Jon among his peers and noticed the glaring differences as he tried to fit in. It was heartbreaking. She would privately cry in her car, pick up the pieces, and then move forward with activities to make him better. The situation completely consumed her; she was like a horse with blinders. Her motto, "short-term pain and long-term gain" so Jon could get better.

Franklin, on the other hand, continued to ask God to heal Jon, but God was not answering his prayers. Then one day, God clearly spoke and said, "Franklin, stop asking me to heal Jon. Love him just the way he is." God's words hit him like a ton of bricks, and he woke up. As he started to reemerge from his deep denial, Franklin began to grieve. He slowly let his dreams for Jon slip away and die. As God began to mend his broken heart, he started to grasp the lifelong situation they were facing and the role he needed to assume as Jon's earthly father and Ruby's husband. It was as if Franklin's heart and mind had been a closed flower bud, which God slowly unfolded and changed over time. He trusted God to construct a new dream for Jon.

"...My grace is sufficient for you, for my power is made
perfect in weakness." 2 Corinthians 12:9 (NIV)

As Franklin re-engaged, the tension with Ruby started to diminish. He began to truly listen to her concerns, fears, and heartbreaks as he took over some of the daily responsibilities. He also started a new tradition. Every Friday he took Jon out to dinner to spend time with him and teach him how to behave in a public setting while providing Ruby with a much-needed break. As Franklin continued to engage, he began to open up and honestly share the pain and sadness he felt regarding Jon and his shattered dreams. Franklin's words and honesty helped Ruby emerge from her depressed state. She was no longer alone on this challenging journey.

As the years passed, Ruby began to quietly celebrate Jon's little accomplishments, even when he achieved things much later than the typical milestones. As he started saying more and more words, she soon realized God was in the middle of the storm with her. He had never abandoned her. Ruby had hope.

Then, a miracle happened. Traveling in a car with Jon was typically an exhausting experience. Sometimes, he would repeat the same five words for forty minutes straight. However, on one special day, the car ride was different. As Jon sat in the back seat, he started to sing the song "I Am a Friend of God." As he sang the song over and over and over again, the powerful words touched her heart and re-energized her tired body. This little boy, who she once feared would never talk, blessed her with his sweet voice singing this powerful song. Yes, Jon is a friend of God and God loves him just the way he is. Ruby believes God was in the car on that extraordinary day and blessed her with an amazing gift. She shared, "God allowed His voice to be heard though Jon." The experience gave her renewed hope, which she desperately needed. God inspired Ruby time and time again through the gift of music. "On some of my lowest days, God re-energized me through powerful music exactly when I needed it."

By the end of elementary school, Jon started to achieve capabilities and skills beyond the expectations of his diagnosis. He began speaking in full sentences, engaging in limited conversations, and reading a few sight words. Then one day, Ruby looked at Jon and realized he was happy. He didn't have any expectations. The socially acceptable expectations came from her, not Jon or God. She understood "social pride" stopped her from releasing the situation entirely to God. Slowly, she started to let go as she trusted God more and more. She was finally able to say the words, "My son has a disability."

Jon is now a teenager and is making remarkable progress in an alternative school for special needs children. They adapt their teaching styles to enhance his learning and comprehension. He still has many challenges facing him, but Ruby no longer worries about milestones. She shared, "Jon has achieved numerous milestones in his own time and in the way God made him."

Life is far more balanced when God is in control. Ruby is living her life again. She now has time to pursue things she enjoys while Franklin continues to be an engaged father. Natalie is exceeding their dreams as she excels in college and enjoys a special bond with her brother. Growing up with a special needs sibling was not easy, but in retrospect, the challenges made her daughter stronger, and God opened her eyes to wonderful opportunities. Natalie is now enjoying improved quality time with her parents that she values immensely.

Ruby shared, "Life is so much simpler when you trust God. During my early journey with Jon, I was exhausted as I tried to lean on my own strength. I was like a hamster on a wheel, running in a vicious circle, trying to fix something that was not broken in God's eyes. I fixated on the world's rules, not God's. I had things backward. Socially acceptable milestones and my worldly pride kept me from turning the situation over to God. It caused a great deal of pain. In retrospect, I regret not reaching out for help and support from my family and friends during my painful journey. I still have tough days, but I now lean on God for my peace. After all, He knows Jon better than anyone. Through my ups and downs, I gained comfort from this powerful Bible verse."

"Be joyful in hope, patient in affliction, faithful in prayer."
Romans 12:12 (NIV)

Franklin added, "God can take the most painful things in your life and use them for good if you will simply surrender to Him. Our Heavenly Father cares about us and our character. He helps us grow as we trust and obey Him. We know there is no cause or effect as to why Jon has the challenges he has, but we do know God is with us as we continue on this journey together. He loves us and is reconstructing our new dream for Jon."

Ruby concluded, "We are on a life-long, faith-filled journey that continues to evolve. Each day presents new challenges, and we don't know what the future holds. We still experience days of grieving, but we are eternally grateful for our amazing daughter and special son. Together, we love Jon and celebrate as he grows and evolves in his own, unique way. We find joy in the hope that Jon will find his passion and fulfill God's purpose for his life."

REFLECTION

1. Have you faced a challenge in your life that completely shattered your hopes and expectations? *Yes / No*

   If you answered yes, what happened? _____

   _____

   _____

   _____

   _____

   How did you feel? _____

   _____

   _____

   _____

   Did you seek God's guidance to "get you through" the situation? *Yes / No*

   If you answered yes, what happened? _____

   _____

   _____

   _____

   _____

2. Pause and Reflect.
   Are you open to allowing God's guidance in your life?
   Yes / No

   _____

   _____

   _____

   _____

NEXT STEPS

1. As we saw in Ruby's story, relinquishing control of a situation and turning it over to God can sometimes be tough when you are in the middle of a storm. Satan wants you to go through storms alone, so you are vulnerable, miserable, and afraid. However, when you choose to "hit the pause button" and seek God's guidance, you unleash His power. God will join you in the middle of your storm. He will never leave your side as He replaces your fear with His peace.

   Are you trying to overcome the storms of your life without God? *Yes / No*

   If you answered yes, what are you trying to accomplish on your own?

   _____

   _____

   _____

   _____

   How can God's guidance help you? _____

   _____

   _____

   _____

   _____

CLOSING PRAYER

   If you are currently in the middle of a storm or need God's help to maneuver through a particular situation, you can ask Him for guidance and clarity right now by praying this simple prayer:

   Dear God,

   I need your help with _____. While this is hard for me, I am turning my situation over to you. Please provide me with insight, clarity, and the help I need to move forward. I am trusting you to strengthen me as I follow your guidance. Thank you for helping me. Amen.

Losing a Child

"The Lord is close to the brokenhearted and saves those who are crushed in spirit." Psalm 34:18 (NIV)

The phone rang. As I slowly picked up the receiver and said hello, I heard a very controlled yet shaken voice of my oldest grandson. "Grandma – there was a bad car wreck. We are heading to where they took Dad. Mom didn't make it". The phone went silent. Then, I heard a loud click. I paused. I thought there must be a mistake; this can't be right. What did he say? Did I actually hear the message? I suddenly felt as though my brain would POP like an over-inflated balloon. "God, Oh God, I prayed, please say this isn't so." As my mind began to clear, I realized it was not my imagination. My worst nightmare became a reality. We lost our cherished child, our dear Laura.

LaNelle, now eighty-seven, and going blind from the effects of macular degeneration, sat quietly at her kitchen table as she continued to share her painful story about the loss of their daughter six years earlier.

Our world as we knew it changed on that hot, fateful day of August. The day began with what might be called a premonition for me. On arising early that morning, I had an indescribable feeling of heaviness, stress, and tragedy—a sense that something devastating was about to happen. I had never experienced such a horrific feeling before. I immediately started praying, but no answers came. As the day wore on, the feeling intensified; I began walking the floor as I tried to figure out what was going on in my mind and body. I continued to pray. What was happening to me? It was a miserable existence with a close description of insanity. In retrospect, I now know God was preparing me to receive the shocking news. When the phone rang late that afternoon, the horrible feelings suddenly stopped and were replaced with shock, disbelief, and uncontrollable sadness.

It was at that moment God stepped in and began to carry my husband and me through our emotional shock, suffering, and yes even anger. God intervened in amazing ways we could have never anticipated throughout the next days, weeks, and months. As our pastor joined us at our home on that Saturday evening of despair, his very presence gave us a sense of peace which is hard to describe. It was as if God's own special emissary was placed at our kitchen table to keep us comforted, when all comfort seemed non-existent. He prayed with us as our immediate attention, hope, and prayers surrounded our son-in-law who was in critical condition. He was air-lifted from the remote desert site of the accident to a Las Vegas hospital where one of the best orthopedic surgeons in America resided. God had interceded.

Details of the tragic head-on car accident began to unfold that evening. We learned that people at the accident scene 120 miles away prayed for our son-in-law and others who had numerous injuries. Laura was killed instantly by a young woman who had been driving recklessly and taking undue chances passing other vehicles. Based on the details regarding the accident and head-on collision, there was no doubt it was Laura's time to leave us. She was loaned to us for a certain amount of time, and that time was now over.

The following week was a foggy blur as we went through the steps to plan a funeral. As demonstrated by over 500 people that attended her memorial service, Laura was loved by many. We laid Laura to rest on a cloudy day at the base of the Sierra Nevada Mountains. It was over, yet our journey was only beginning.

After the graveside service and our tearful goodbyes, we slowly got in our car for the three-hour drive home. God continued to be with us. We noticed an amazing rainbow over the eastern White Mountains. It was particularly special because it had not rained that day. As we drove across the Mojave Desert, the rainbow continued to follow us mile after mile. It became a topic of discussion in the car. Sometimes the rainbow would become a double rainbow, then transition back to one rainbow. It was just breathtaking. For nearly three hours, the rainbow remained with us. As we approached our highway turnoff to head west, the rainbow suddenly became vibrant, and then burst in the sky like a bright explosion. It was as if Laura was saying goodbye...let the party begin!

Despite the numerous signs which clearly demonstrated God was with us on our healing journey, the following days and weeks were pure agony. I had never experienced such a profound heartbreak and emotional pain. I did my best to remain faithful in my Bible reading and prayer life, but it was difficult. "God, why our beloved Laura, why?" I was angry and resentful of this woman who took Laura away from us.

It was at this time God again intervened. My friends embraced me, helped me, and prayed for me when I could no longer find the words to pray. I was paralyzed with grief. They could see the anger and resentment I carried around like a ball and chain; the anger was smothering me. These dear friends asked God to help me move forward, and yes, with God's grace, enable me to forgive this young woman who recklessly killed my daughter.

As the weeks progressed, I began to function on a day to day basis. I was grateful. I soon began to explore and discuss my desire to forgive this woman. Some people thought I was crazy, stating I should seek revenge as a way to heal. Throw her in jail, go after money! However, as a Christian woman, I knew forgiveness was a necessary next step for me, but it was extremely hard. My heart was shattered. How could I let go of my anger and resentment? I needed a power greater than me; I could not do this alone. I needed God to help me forgive. As the Bible verse states, Jesus forgives us, and we need to forgive others:

"Do not judge, and you will not be judged.
Do not condemn, and you will not be condemned.
Forgive, and you will be forgiven." Luke 6:37 (NIV)

As the weeks passed on, my husband and I decided to go on our annual trip to visit family and friends across the country. However, this year's trip to see the changing leaves in the northeast was unique and special. At nearly every stop, we found ourselves enjoying the reassuring company of other parents and friends who had lost a child. It was quite honestly astonishing. We could not believe what was happening. God provided us with example after example of people who lost a child, picked up the pieces, and moved forward with their lives through the grace of God. It was what we needed at the exact time we needed it. There was hope, and we knew our hope was in Jesus! It was evident that God's hand was embracing our lives and providing the comfort we desperately sought.

Through the strength and love given by God, I was finally able to forgive the woman who killed Laura. To have the burden and anger released from my heart was indescribable–another gift from God. I now know firsthand the power of forgiveness. I still have extreme sadness about the loss of Laura, but I no longer carry the anger and resentment that exhausted me.

I was blessed with the opportunity to write a letter to the woman responsible for the accident. I shared that I forgave her. I let her know that it was my hope she would remember that prayer changes things and God will always walk beside her. I was also granted the opportunity to write a letter to the judge who was presiding over the accident case.

Due to the severity of the accident, the driver was charged with manslaughter. On the day of sentencing, I understand the packed courtroom was extremely emotional. My husband and I chose not to attend. Fifty-four letters were sent to the judge, but only one was read in court that day—my letter. It clearly stated we forgave this young woman and pleaded she be spared from prison as she had suffered enough; we requested community service instead. God again intervened, and the judge fulfilled our request.

God continues to be our strength! We lost Laura through a tragic accident. She was a precious little jewel that was loaned to us and taken away too soon. We all need to be careful never to allow a tragedy to steal our joy and love. Resentment and hatred only hurt the person bearing those feelings. Forgiveness is for both the giver and receiver. Through our story, it is my hope and prayer that others will lean on God and receive or give the gift of forgiveness! We praise God every day for the time we had with Laura. God graciously surrounds us with strength and love day after day.

Laura

Laura's Mom LaNelle

REFLECTION

1. Pause and Reflect.
    Are you angry or disappointed about something in your life?
    Yes / No

    If you answered yes, what are you angry or disappointed about?

    _____

    _____

    _____

    _____

2. How does your anger or disappointment(s) make you feel?

    _____

    _____

    _____

    _____

3. Who is benefiting from your feelings of anger and disappointment?

    _____

4. Has anyone ever forgiven you? *Yes / No*
    If you answered yes, how did it make you feel?

    _____

    _____

    _____

    _____

NEXT STEPS

1. Do you want to forgive someone? *Yes / No*
   If you answered yes, who do you want to forgive?

   _____

   _____

   _____

   _____

2. What positive things might happen if you forgive this person?

   _____

   _____

   _____

   _____

3. What is stopping you from forgiving someone? Be completely honest with yourself. Fill in the blanks that relate to you and your situation.

   I am angry because _____

   _____

   _____

   _____

   I am hurt because _____

   _____

   _____

   _____

   I am confused because _____

   _____

_____

_____

_____

4. With God's help, do you want to release your anger and hurt?
    Yes / No

    Do you want to forgive the person or people that you listed
    above? *Yes / No*

    If you answered yes, slowly read <u>each</u> of your concerns in Step 3,
    then add the following phrase:

    *Lord, help me to let go of this feeling. I am trusting you to free me
    from this anger and hurt – I cannot do it on my own. Through your
    power, please help me to forgive* _____.

    Thank you. Amen.

CLOSING PRAYER

Dear God,

*Thank you for caring about all areas of my life. Please help me to
remember that you are a powerful and loving God. You can and will
help me change the way I think and feel about situations. Thank
you for the gift of forgiveness. Amen!*

Living Through Abandonment

*"You intended to harm me, but God intended it
for good to accomplish what is now being done,
the saving of many lives." Genesis 50:20 (NIV)*

Franklin was living the lifestyle of the rich and famous. From all outward appearances, this eighteen-year-old had it all – from his BMW to his luxury apartment, expensive clothes, wild parties, and lots of women. Yes! He had finally arrived, and life was going great, or was it? As he strived to maintain his affluent facade, it became apparent he was living way beyond his means. Unpaid bills started to accumulate month after month, and his financial pressures were mounting day after day. To make matters worse, his extensive partying reached a level where alcohol now tasted good. Then, it happened. Investigators discovered he had embezzled from the company where he worked for the past two years. He was fired immediately, and his house of cards came tumbling down. His life fell apart, or maybe it was just beginning.

Franklin and his twin were born three months premature in the 1960s. He weighed slightly over a pound and was not expected to live due to multiple issues. Given the dire situation, the doctors bypassed his birth certificate name, and he was called Baby B. Against all the odds, both he and his sister survived, but he faced many health, physical, and "learning" challenges for several years.

When Franklin was finally released from the hospital, his tough life was just beginning. His twenty-one-year-old mother was

LIVING THROUGH ABANDONMENT

unwed and already had four other children at home. She was not interested in nurturing children, let alone caring for two needy premature babies. In fact, she tried to miscarry the twins before their birth. By age three, Social Services intervened, took the twins away from their mother, and placed them in foster care. God protected them and began to prepare Franklin for his future.

Franklin lived with his first set of foster parents for five years. He was extremely happy living with the pastor and his wife, who he called Mom and Dad. It was a real home, and Franklin felt safe. He started to learn about the Bible and attended Sunday School and church every week. They taught him right from wrong. They also helped him with his physical issues due to his slightly deformed legs and encouraged him as he tackled his learning challenges. He felt loved.

Then at age eight, the unthinkable happened. Social Services pulled the twins out of foster care and returned them to their biological mother and father who had recently married. Franklin was afraid. For the next nine months, he lived in a cold, negative house with parents and siblings that were basically strangers. He felt out-of-place, unloved, and unwanted. Domestic violence was a common occurrence including physical fights, cursing, and screaming. When the screaming would start, Franklin would find a place to hide, close his eyes, and cover his ears, doing his best to block out the violence.

One day, without warning or discussion, his mother threw his clothes into a trash bag and placed him in the car with his twin sister. They drove about ten minutes until they reached his foster parents' home. As she pulled the kids out of the car, they held on tightly to their trash bags; the trash bags that contained all their belongings. She knocked on the door, rang the doorbell, then looked down at the nine-year-old twins and said, "Here's where you want to be." She turned around and walked away, leaving the kids standing all alone.

Franklin was thrilled to be back with his mom and dad. He once again felt safe and loved. Life was great for the next year until Good Friday. His mom was going to get dessert and said, "Do you want apple pie or peach pie?" These were the last words he ever heard her speak. As she was making her way up the steps after returning from the grocery store, she accidentally slipped, hit her head, and then fell into a coma. She died at noon on Easter Sunday. The last time he saw his mom, she was in a casket. Despite the pastor's attempts to keep the twins, Social Services refused to leave them with only one adult. The twins were transitioned to another foster home.

Franklin's second set of foster parents provided the twins with a positive environment in a Christian home. They were unable to have their own children, so they chose to extend their love to over 100 foster children during their lifetime. Franklin and his sister were two of the fortunate children to live in their home. His dad was the "most loving father in the world." He was optimistic and reassuring. While his mom enforced discipline and rules, she also provided positive reinforcement and encouragement. She would tell Franklin he was going to be great; words that followed him as he became an adult. The twins thrived in the hopeful and loving environment.

It was during this time that Franklin was finally able to transition from his leg braces and "pilgrim shoes" into his first pair of real shoes; he was so excited. Franklin endured many years of kids making fun of him due to his physical challenges. He still had many learning challenges to overcome, but he was happy.

When Franklin was twelve years old, his foster parents initiated adoption papers. During the adoption process, the state uncovered that his birthmother deceived Social Services. She claimed his biological father abandoned the family and she was unable to care for the twins. However, when his birth father was notified, he stopped the adoption process since he never left the family or their home. Social Services forced the kids to return to their biological parents since they no longer qualified for foster care. Franklin was devastated. He once again was required to leave loving parents. He was sad and heartbroken.

From age thirteen until graduation, Franklin and his sister lived in the dysfunctional home of his biological parents. Drama, yelling, physical fighting, and favoritism was the foundation of the house. There was no love or respect. It was during this time that an uncle showed a special interest in Franklin and sexually abused him. Franklin was struggling both personally and in school. When his mother saw his sixth-grade report card, she said, "You are never going to amount to anything. You are just going to be a loser." He was devastated. To make matters worse, the kids at school were making fun of him because he stuttered. His situation was further complicated due to his walking issues, reading challenges, learning disabilities, and eye issues.

Fortunately, Franklin soon realized there was a multi-cultural church just up the street. Attending church gave him a reason to escape the drama in his house and bullying at school. The church members gladly accepted him just the way he was and quickly became his strength and escape from reality. The pastors were a great source of encouragement. A few moms and dads at the church embraced him as part of their extended family. He joined the Bible quizzing team, cleaned the church, and became very active in the youth group. He felt loved once again. It was here, at age thirteen, he accepted Jesus as his personal savior.

Life moved on as the drama and violence in his house intensified, and the church family continued to be his refuge. Then one day, as he was praying during a church service, the most astounding thing happened. Time seemed to stand still as God clearly spoke to him saying, "Franklin, I want you to become a pastor." God then followed up with a Bible verse that was Franklin's call to the ministry:

"...Truly I tell you, whatever you did for one of the least
of these brothers and sisters of mine, you did for me."
Matthew 25:40 (NIV)

At the end of the church service, a woman came up, touched his shoulder, then quietly said, "God told me you had been called to be a pastor and you need to listen." Franklin was shocked, and he felt conflicted. He did not want to become a pastor; yes, pastors were kind and loving people, but they did not make a lot of money. So, he chose to ignore the call from God and moved forward.

At age sixteen, Franklin made a pivotal decision to run his own life. He set his sights on the lifestyles of the rich and famous. While trying to keep one foot in the church, he started to spread his wings in the world and dabble with the sinful things in life. Franklin sought self-worth and acceptance in material things rather than God. He thought he had it all figured out. He could be in the church while enjoying all the things the world had to offer. "If I can go to school and become a successful businessman, then I can make more money than a minister and give a larger tithe to help the church. Everyone wins."

Franklin began working at a pizza parlor where he was quickly promoted to a shift manager due to his strong work ethic. He soon transitioned to another company and rapidly worked his way up from a stock boy to a manager. By age eighteen, he was making a good salary; he liked the money. When he graduated from high school, Franklin immediately moved out of his biological parents' house. He was confident he had things all figured out. Life was looking good, or so he thought.

With his sights fixated on an upper-class lifestyle, Franklin managed to transition into a luxury apartment and a used BMW. His new life was flashy, high-end, and fast paced. He was styling in designer clothes and partying hard every night. People wanted to be like him for the first time in his life. He liked the attention versus "a person that had been thrown away with the trash."

Franklin quickly discovered he could use credit cards and overspend without feeling much impact. Then, reality started to set in. Unpaid bills began to pile up, and creditors started to call. He realized he was in trouble with no clear recovery path if he wanted to preserve his showy facade.

The pressure from creditors continued to mount as his life began to spiral out of control. Then one day, Franklin decided to compromise one of his foundational values. He stole a few dollars from his company to pay his bills, thinking no one would notice. Before he knew it, he embezzled thousands of dollars. One day, his district manager came to visit and asked him to join a security meeting, which in reality was a meeting with investigators. He was caught. His embezzling scheme was busted, and he was immediately fired. His world came crashing down.

Franklin was devastated and depressed. His flashy world fell apart, and he was flat broke. His belongings were repossessed. One night, out of pure despair, he became extremely drunk and passed out in his apartment. His sister happened to be visiting and heard him throwing up in his sleep. She turned his head to one side so that he could breathe. Had she not been in his apartment that night, he would have suffocated in his own vomit. He had indeed hit rock bottom.

The next morning, he awoke to God's voice in his head clearly saying, "Franklin, how's running your life going?" Franklin, now realizing he was covered in vomit, actually answered and said, "It is going terribly. I messed up my life." He then stopped and realized he was running away from God's request to go into the ministry. He was trying to find self-worth and acceptance in things rather than God. It was his "ah-ha" moment. He then clearly said, "Okay. I will go into the ministry," and he asked God for forgiveness.

Franklin's decision that morning changed his life forever. He realized God saved him from drowning in his vomit and despair. As he began trusting God with his life, positive things started to happen. His former employer decided not to call the police or pursue felony charges. The only requirement made was that he repay the stolen money. He knew God handled the situation. And this was only the beginning.

The Sunday after his decision to go into the ministry, Franklin asked his pastor if he could address the church congregation. For thirty minutes during the Sunday morning service, he stood up and with complete transparency, confessed the double life he had been living. Franklin stated he pretended to be a devout Christian, but he was not. He disclosed the embezzlement and the fact that he was fired and lost everything. He asked his church family to forgive him and was relieved when the church embraced him with love, compassion, and forgiveness.

As he prepared to leave the church that morning, a gentleman approached him and said he was aware of a job opening. Franklin knew this was not a coincidence. God was creating a new path for him. Within a week, he started a new job working in a Christian bookstore where he enjoyed employment for the next two years and paid off his embezzlement debts. The store owner was an influential mentor for Franklin and supported him as he pulled his life together.

Then one day as he was working, God spoke to Franklin stating he needed to attend college and prepare to be a minister. God went on to say, "If you go to college, I will pay for it." Now, Franklin trusted God and wanted to be obedient, but he had his doubts. However, trusting God, he applied to a private Christian school and was accepted for the fall semester. He still had no idea how to pay the $12,000 annual tuition but kept trusting God. His church family gave him $700 as he prepared to leave for college and his supportive boss gave him $1000.

At age twenty-one, Franklin loaded his limited belongings into the church van, and one of his church dads drove him to college. He was excited but understandably apprehensive. When he arrived at the freshman check-in area, he soon learned he did not have a dorm room. He immediately felt abandoned, just like he did as a child. Then God spoke to him clearly once again saying, "Don't worry about this. I know you feel abandoned, but I have a plan for you. I am going to use the bad stuff in your life for my honor and glory." Then Franklin remembered a key Bible verse that gave him hope:

> "For I know the plans I have for you," declares the Lord,
> "plans to prosper you and not to harm you, plans to
> give you hope and a future." Jeremiah 29:11 (NIV)

It was on this day, at that time, the ugly puzzle pieces of Franklin's life started to mold together for something bigger than he could imagine. A room became available and was assigned to Franklin. As he moved into his college dorm room, his abandonment issues suddenly came to a close. He finally grasped that God was with him no matter what. He realized God loved him, despite his parents' lack of love. He understood God's love was unconditional, even though he took wrong paths.

From that point forward, his issues and feeling of "not being good enough" just disappeared. Thanks to God's amazing grace, Franklin's eyes were now wide open to the possibilities of his life in the ministry serving God. As the day came to a close, he recalled a Bible passage that gave him great comfort:

Romans 8:31-39 (NIV)

What, then, shall we say in response to these things? If God is for us, who can be against us? He who did not spare his own Son, but gave him up for us all—how will he not also, along with him, graciously give us all things? Who will bring any charge against those whom God has chosen? It is God who justifies. Who then is the one who condemns? No one. Christ Jesus who died—more than that, who was raised to life—is at the right hand of God and is also interceding for us.

Who shall separate us from the love of Christ? Shall trouble or hardship or persecution or famine or nakedness or danger or sword? As it is written: "For your sake we face death all day long; we are considered as sheep to be slaughtered." No, in all these things we are more than conquerors through him who loved us. For I am convinced that neither death nor life, neither angels nor demons, neither the present nor the future, nor any powers, neither height nor depth, nor anything else in all creation, will be able to separate us from the love of God that is in Christ Jesus our Lord.

Franklin went on to graduate with a double major. As promised, God ensured all his college expenses were covered. He has now enjoyed over twenty-five years in the ministry serving the Lord. He married the love of his life and was blessed with two children. As promised, God took the worst things in his life and used them for good. He has a personal passion focused on helping foster children understand that God loves them no matter what has transpired in their lives. Through God's grace, Franklin was able to share unconditional love with both of his biological parents, something he never thought was possible. He learned firsthand that with God, all things are possible. Praise God!

REFLECTION

1. Close your eyes and spend a few minutes reflecting on your life, from childhood to present. During the good times and the tough times of your life, how has God "shown-up" to help you? Take a moment and write down the specific things and events that come to your mind.

_____

_____

_____

_____

_____

_____

_____

2. How has God blessed your life in the last 30 days? In the space below, write down those blessings and thank God for each one.

_____

_____

_____

_____

_____

_____

_____

NEXT STEPS

1. Have things happened in your life that left you confused, angry, or bitter? List those events/things on the next page. As you list each item, ask God to remove that burden from your heart and mind, and replace it with the warmth of His love and peace.

_____

_____

_____

_____

_____

2. The bookstore owner helped Franklin as he pulled his life back to-gether. Do you know someone who could use your help? List their name(s) below, then add one thing you will do to help that person in the next seven days.

NAME	ACTION

CLOSING PRAYER

Dear God,

Thank you for helping me during the good and bad times of my life. Thank you for helping me land on my feet when I have made bad decisions. Please help me to pay attention to your guidance and to be obedient as I strive to fulfill your plan for my life. Thank you for all my blessings and your unconditional love. I love you. Amen.

Losing a Spouse

*"But they that wait upon the Lord shall renew their
strength; they shall mount up with wings as eagles;
they shall run, and not be weary; and they
shall walk, and not faint." Isaiah 40:31 (KJV)*

It was a hot August day in the middle of the Mojave Desert. Barb's husband of fifty-four years was now in a nursing home to receive 24/7 care. His condition was declining quickly. Barb and her daughters were exhausted from the trips to and from the nursing facility and decided to rest before returning that evening. Suddenly, her eldest daughter sat straight up from a deep sleep and loudly exclaimed, "We need to go see Dad now!" She threw on her shoes, grabbed her keys, and headed for the front door. Barb tried to calm her determined daughter, but there was no rationalizing with her. She had an urgent need to be at her father's bedside. They followed her lead and rushed to the car.

Upon arrival at Dan's room, it was clear he had taken a turn for the worse. Barb gently placed her hand over his, then carefully stroked his hair as her girls surrounded the bed. She lovingly yet firmly told him it was okay to go to heaven now; he was tired, and it was time to let go. With that, Dan took his last breath and passed away.

As Barb sadly walked out of Dan's room for the last time, she realized it was not a coincidence they arrived an hour early. God ensured her family was with Dan, so he did not pass away alone. He was faithful to her once again. In fact, God had been her daily source of strength for the last several years as she supported Dan through strokes, heart attacks, and diabetes. She would now need to lean on God for strength like never before as she entered the next phase of her life as a widow. Barb firmly believed God would provide comfort as she relied on her faith. She was reassured by the Bible verse below:

"Blessed are those who mourn, for they will be comforted."
Matthew 5:4 (NIV)

Sixteen years have now passed since her husband's death. Barb, now eighty-eight, paused to reflect on her relationship with Dan and the strength God has provided. "I am incredibly sad Dan is no longer with me to enjoy the kids and grandkids, but I am so grateful for the time we had together. He was a strong, thoughtful family man that embraced life and his community. He was my best friend. We met in 1943 during a freshman English class, but never dated. After high school, he joined the Navy. We reconnected in January of 1948 and enjoyed our first date on Valentine's Day — the same day we decided to spend the rest of our lives together. It was simply meant to be."

Reflecting on his illness, Barb shared, "It is hard to watch someone you love die in inches as physical abilities slip away." She mourned Dan's losses daily—the basic simple things that we take for granted he could no longer do — from combing his hair to brushing his teeth to feeding himself. When she lovingly washed his face, he would smile and say he loved her. "Together, through the power of daily and sometimes hourly prayer, God gave us the strength to move forward, reflect on our memories, and enjoy being together."

The day of Dan's funeral was uplifting and amazing. Over 500 people were packed into the church that day; people who he silently touched in positive ways through random acts of kindness and generosity. As his casket was carried out of the church, the organ played loudly "Fight On"; his favorite USC fight song. "Fight On" remains Barb's motto as she leans on God for her daily strength.

Barb believes God asked her to devote the rest of her life to fulfilling Dan's passion for fighting polio in third world countries and helping teens attend college via scholarships. Through God's strength and Rotary International, she focused her sadness into positive energy to make a difference. She helped raise over $350,000 for teens to attend college and over $35,000 toward the elimination of polio throughout the world.

Barb went on to share, "God is my rock. He eases my pain and loneliness, puts His loving arms around me, and comforts me every day. I can feel his presence. At night when I am all alone, I slowly shut off each light in the house, sit on the side of my bed to read the Bible, then pray for God's strength, safekeeping, and guidance." She paused for a moment to reflect, and then said, "With God's help, you can climb your way out of sadness into the light by leaning on Him for strength...simply trust God with all your heart and seek Him first."

> *"Seek ye first the kingdom of God, and his righteousness; and all these things shall be added unto you."*
> *Matthew 6:33 (KJV)*

Barb faithfully follows her 4Ps on a daily basis:

- Pray—You do not need to use fancy words, just talk to God

- Purposely read the Bible

- Praise God—Thank Him for Jesus and the Holy Spirit that lives within you

- Participate in at least one random act of kindness every day

Love, hope, happiness, goodness, and strength all come from God. If you find yourself mourning the loss of a special person in your life, you can move forward if you rely on Him as your source of strength. Ask God to help you by praying, "Dear Lord, please give me the strength to move forward." Trust Him! Yes, it truly is that simple.

Barb closed her thoughts by saying, "I enjoyed fifty-four years of marriage and am comforted by my wonderful memories of Dan. In fact, I wear his wedding ring on a necklace around my neck, so it is close to my heart at all times. God gave me the strength to move forward after Dan passed away – He will also help you!"

Live the life God wants you to live – finish running the race! With God in your corner, you can't lose. Fight On!

Dan – 1948

Dan and Barb – 1995

REFLECTION

1. Have you lost someone special in your life? If yes, who have you lost?

_____

_____

_____

_____

_____

2. Are you still mourning your loss? *Yes / No*

   If you answered yes, how is your sadness impacting your life?

_____

_____

_____

_____

_____

NEXT STEPS

1. People mourn in various ways and in different timeframes. If you find yourself paralyzed by grief, reach out to your local church or counseling center and ask for help. There are excellent grief support groups to help you on your journey.

_____

_____

_____

_____

_____

_____

2. What positive things could happen if you trust God and ask Him for the strength, guidance, and wisdom to move forward from your loss?

_____

_____

_____

_____

_____

3. As we saw in Barb's story, she chose to move forward and honor Dan by continuing to support charities and causes that were important to him. Her proactive actions helped her healing process. Pause and reflect. Is there a charity or cause that you can support in memory of your loved one?

_____

_____

_____

_____

_____

CLOSING PRAYER

Dear God,

Thank you for meeting me where I am today. You know my heart and the pain that I am feeling. Please help me to move forward as I trust and depend on you for strength and wisdom. Thank you! Amen.

Beating Stage 4 Cancer

"A man with leprosy came and knelt before him and said, "Lord, if you are willing, you can make me clean." Jesus reached out his hand and touched the man. "I am willing," he said. "Be clean!" Immediately he was cleansed of his leprosy." Matthew 8:2-3 (NIV)

"It's cancer. Your liver is full of tumors. There are also tumors in your spleen and the base of your esophagus." Then the doctor clearly stated, "If you have liver cancer, most likely the oncologist will tell you to close out your life, you will be gone by Christmas." Al was shocked. It was October 23rd and Christmas was only eight weeks away.

Al's miraculous journey began five years earlier in the fall of 2003. He and his wife Kate had been working with an adoption agency for nearly two years in their quest to adopt a child and give their daughter Mary a little brother or sister. One Sunday morning, as he sat by Kate during a church service, the priest read a Bible verse from the book of Mark:

"Whoever welcomes one of these little children in my name welcomes me; and whoever welcomes me does not welcome me but the one who sent me." Mark 9:37 (NIV)

This verse prepared their hearts for a call that came a few weeks later asking if they would accept the adoption of a little boy who was born prematurely. They were thrilled and jumped at the opportunity to welcome Henry into their family. They knew God blessed them with a special gift and they were grateful.

During this time, Al who was a colonel in the Army received transfer orders to Hawaii with a report date of July 2004. The timeline for the family's move aligned perfectly with the finalization of Henry's adoption. The only issue regarding the transfer was their realization a few months after the move that Hawaii lacked the specialized care their daughter Mary required for her degenerative kidney disease. As the months went on, there were indications she was not receiving adequate medical care, and they were concerned.

Al and Kate prayed for God's guidance and direction regarding the next steps they should take for their family and Mary's medical care. Amazingly, the answer came quickly and clearly. Without hesitation, they took a leap of faith and trusted God for the next phase of their life. By June 2006, everything fell into place. Al retired from the Army, and they moved to Raleigh, NC to be close to major medical centers. This move to Raleigh, however, would prove to have more significance than they could ever realize.

Al did not have a job or any professional network when they moved to Raleigh. Despite his unemployment, he was at complete peace and enjoyed working on their new home. He knew they made the right decision and God was guiding them. Within six months, Al landed an excellent job with a small business owner who truly cared about his employees. Life was great, but the job turned out to be far more demanding than he hoped or anticipated.

The months passed by quickly. By the spring of 2008, Al found himself working up to seven days a week to fulfill the demands as the Vice President of Operations. His life was out of balance mentally, physically, and spiritually. He knew he was not devoting the time he should to his family and it bothered him.

The spring moved to summer, and Al continued to be consumed by work and deadlines. In September, he noticed he was not feeling right. He lost his appetite and Maalox became a staple in his diet. His clothes were getting loose, and he was dropping weight without trying. Despite his symptoms, he pushed forward and did not slow down. Kate was concerned and urged him to see a doctor, but Al insisted he had too much work to do and could not afford the interruption. By October, his weight loss was apparent, and he felt terrible. He was responsible for a major corporate planning session later that month, so he continued to push forward. He had no idea of the storm that was brewing just a few days away.

It was at this point Kate decided to take control of Al's health situation.

- Sunday, October 19th – Kate informed Al he had an appointment with a gastroenterologist at 8 AM the next morning. She shared the doctor's office was on his way to work, and he would need to pay for the appointment if he did not show up. The corporate planning session was that week, but Al knew he was getting worse. He could no longer eat, and the sight of food made him feel sick. So, he decided to go to the appointment.

- Monday, October 20th – The doctor informed Al that something did not feel right in his abdomen, so he scheduled an ultrasound for the next day.

- Wednesday, October 22nd – The doctor did not like the results of his ultrasound, and Al's liver did not look good. A magnetic resonance imaging (MRI) scan was scheduled for the next morning. Al and Kate were concerned. In the back of Al's mind was the fact that cancer killed his father and grandfather.

- Thursday, October 23rd – Within a few hours of the MRI scan, Al received a call from the doctor with the results.

He said there were tumors all over his liver, in his spleen, and at the base of his esophagus. "It is cancer, and we do not know the source." Both Al and Kate were numb. They did not know what to do, what to say, or where to turn. It was surreal, like being in a free-fall. An appointment was scheduled to meet with an oncologist on Friday. As they started to reach out to family and friends, everyone began to pray.

- Friday, October 24th – Al awoke with clarity regarding his next step. "Why don't I call Sasha?" he thought. She was a renowned oncologist at Mother Frances Hospital in Tyler, Texas and a close family friend. At about the same time, Kate walked in and said, "Al, we need to call Sasha." They soon learned Al's mom had the same thought. After a short phone call, they learned Sasha wanted to see him the next day. This was positive news as his oncologist in Raleigh indicated there would be a two-week delay before he could have additional tests conducted. Al did not have that kind of time.

- On this same day, Al received an amazing gift of encouragement from his boss. He informed Al that his job description was changed to "Get Better." He went on to state, "If anything happens, we will take care of your family." Al was overwhelmed with this kind and generous gesture. It touched his heart.

- Saturday, October 25th – Al and Kate flew to Dallas. He was immediately taken to the hospital for a physical and a complete panel of blood tests.

- Sunday, October 26th – The hospital conducted a full battery of tests including a fluoroscopy directed biopsy.

- Monday, October 27th – Sasha convened a Board of Doctors to review the results and determine if other tests were required so they could rapidly identify the source of the cancer and move forward with a treatment plan.

- Wednesday, October 29th – Less than one week from his original diagnosis, Sasha completed the comprehensive findings and treatment plan. The good news, he had Stage 4 Non-Hodgkin's Lymphoma. The liver was not the source of his cancer. The bad news, it was a very aggressive type of cancer and time was of the essence. The cells were multiplying rapidly. Treatment had to begin immediately.

- Thursday, October 30th – They inserted a power port into Al's chest in preparation for chemo treatments.

- Friday, October 31st – Al kept a positive attitude as he received his first dosage of chemo; administered by Sister Silvia, a wonderful oncology nurse. He remained in the hospital that night so they could monitor his vital signs and assess his reaction to the chemo.

- Saturday, November 1st – Sasha informed Al she would transition his case over to her former boss and mentor. He was the Chief of Hematology-Oncology at Duke University. Duke was only forty minutes from his home in Raleigh, NC. It was an amazing coincidence, or was it?

- Monday, November 3rd – Al and Kate flew home just in time to vote and celebrate his daughter's birthday. His chemo treatments continued on November 14th and the day before Thanksgiving.

As Al's medical whirlwind continued, there was a miraculous stage being set that only God could orchestrate. When Al returned from Texas, he received an amazing book in the mail written by Dodie Osteen, Joel Osteen's mother, called Healed of Cancer. He started to faithfully read the healing Bible verses that were detailed in the book three times a day. They comforted him. He also prayed and asked God to forgive him for all his sins and to cleanse his soul. He was completely humble before the Lord. Finally, he believed with his whole heart, soul, and mind that God would heal him; he believed at a deeper level than he ever thought was possible. He surrendered his entire life to God. Al was "all in!"

As the month of November progressed, Al was anointed with oil during a healing sacrament performed by his faith-filled priest. Each time he left the church, he would go up to the statue of Jesus, touch his cloak, and then with overflowing faith reflect on the following Bible verse:

> "When she heard about Jesus, she came up behind him
> in the crowd and touched his cloak, because she thought,
> "If I touch his clothes, I will be healed."
> Mark 5:27-28 (NIV)

Then, one evening in late November, Al was quietly resting in his bed. He was extremely sick, very thin, and completely bald from the chemo treatments. He just finished reading the healing Bible verses and saying his evening prayer when his little son Henry came into his room, gently climbed into his bed, and fell asleep.

As Al watched Henry peacefully sleeping, he reflected on their adoption journey and the powerful Bible verse (Mark 9:37) that God provided five years earlier. Then Al thought, "Mark 9:37 says, when we welcomed Henry into our family, we welcomed Jesus, and when we welcomed Jesus, we welcomed God Himself. Why would God allow the adoption to happen the way it did only to have Henry lose his dad to cancer? It just did not make sense."

At that point, Al realized God did not have plans for him to succumb to cancer. He decided to assume the faith of a mustard seed and boldly prayed, "God, you know I want to get better. I will never ask you to heal me again. I believe you will heal me. I will only thank you for making me better." After he confidently prayed, his human mind thought, "But it sure would be nice to have a sign that I am healed."

With that thought, Henry, who was sound asleep, rolled on his side, put his hand over Al's heart, took a deep breath, and exhaled a huge sigh across his dad's chest. Al believes it was God using Henry to breathe directly on him. At that precise moment, Al had an intense tingling that began at the top of his head, rolled down his body, and exited at his toes. In that split second, he knew God had healed him. He then got out of bed, went downstairs, looked at Kate and said, "I'm better." As she looked into his eyes and listened, she immediately believed. Kate's faith in God's word and His promises were a tremendous inspiration to Al throughout his journey.

For the next two weeks, Al and Kate praised and thanked God for his healing. During this same time, Kate had a vision of the doctor walking into his office wearing a white lab coat with a specific tie, holding Al's chart under his arm, smiling and saying, "Great News."

At Al's December chemo appointment, the doctor decided to run another PET-CT scan to review the status of his tumors before administering his fourth chemo treatment. Then, it happened! As they were waiting for the results, the doctor walked into his office exactly as Kate envisioned. The doctor went on to say, "Great News, there is no abnormal activity." Al's cancer was gone. There were holes where the tumors had been located.

Before they had time to celebrate, they realized Al was turning yellow from jaundice right before their eyes. The doctor feared Al was going into liver failure and immediately put him in the hospital. However, things were not as they appeared. The tumors dissolved at the same time and his liver was on overload as it attempted to cleanse his body of the toxins. While in the hospital, one of the doctors told Kate there was no explanation for Al's sudden healing. Kate corrected him, and confidently said, "thanks be to God."

Kate prayed Al would be home in time to celebrate Christmas with the family. One of the nurses told Kate there was no way this would happen. Kate looked at her and said, "Al will be home for Christmas." After about five days in the hospital and blood transfusions to assist his liver with the cleansing process, Al was discharged at 3 PM on Christmas Eve.

Al has now been cancer free for eight years. He values the gift of life and thankfully embraces each new day with his family. He faithfully looks for opportunities to share his story so others can hear about God's amazing grace, power, and unconditional love. In closing, he shared, "Live by faith, not by what you see. Don't be afraid to believe in God. Miracles are for everyone. It can happen to you, but you must completely believe."

Al with his family in 2016

REFLECTION

1. Sometimes our priorities get confused due to the pressures of our day-to-day lives. How many times have you thought or said, "I will take care of that tomorrow." The reality is that none of us are guaranteed we will be here tomorrow. As the Bible states:

    "Why, you do not even know what will happen tomorrow.
    What is your life? You are a mist that appears for
    a little while and then vanishes." James 4:14 (NIV)

    Are you willing to take an in-depth look at your life and your priorities? *Yes / No*

    If yes, find a quiet place where you will not be disturbed as you spend some time reflecting. Ask God to search your heart as you honestly answer the questions below.

    a. Do you know what God's purpose is for your life? Have you asked him?

    _____

    _____

    _____

    _____

    _____

    _____

    b. Do you have your priorities in the right order? If not, what do you need to change or adjust?

    _____

    _____

    _____

    _____

    _____

    _____

c. Are there things in your life you need to stop?

_____

_____

_____

_____

_____

d. Are there things you need to start?

_____

_____

_____

_____

_____

e. Do you need to forgive someone? If yes, who?

_____

_____

_____

_____

f. Do you need to ask someone to forgive you? If yes, who?

_____

_____

_____

_____

_____

g. Do you have any regrets in your life? If yes, what are they? Are there steps can you take to correct these regrets?

_____

_____

_____

_____

_____

_____

h. When was the last time you read the Bible? _____

When was the last time you devoted time to pray? _____

NEXT STEPS

Now Take Action — The power is in your follow-through!

Based on your answers above, are you willing to change something in your life this week? In the next 30 days? In the next 12 months?

The template on the following page is provided to list the things you want to change in your life. Take some time and fill it out!

CLOSING PRAYER

Dear God,

Thank you for my life and for loving me. I want to fulfill your purpose and plans for my life. Please guide and direct me as I move forward. Amen.

MY ACTION PLAN

Action	Start Date	Due Date
This Week		
1.		
2.		
3.		
4.		
5.		
6.		
7.		
Next 30 Days		
1.		
2.		
3.		
4.		
5.		
6.		
7.		
Next 12 Months		
1.		
2.		
3.		
4.		
5.		
6.		
7.		

Living with Dementia –
A Caregiver's Journey

"Trust in the Lord with all your heart and lean not on your own understanding; In all your ways submit to him, and he will make your paths straight." Proverbs 3: 5-6 (NIV)

Mom was changing. At first, there were the subtle indicators and simple things such as forgetting names, confusing details, and getting disoriented in the kitchen. I knew she was getting a little older, so the changes were to be expected. I was completely unaware that Mom was working hard to mask her early symptoms of dementia. I had no idea that a devastating, yet very special journey lay ahead. I quickly learned firsthand, if you truly trust God, He will carry you through the difficult times in your life.

Mary Lee was a vibrant lady who deeply loved God and her family. While she stood only 5'3" tall, she was a strong and focused woman. She was the mother of six children who spanned across eighteen years of age, an amazing cook, incredible hostess, a loyal friend, and dedicated servant to our Lord. She always looked for people who required extra care and seniors that just needed a friend. To say it simply, Mary Lee was a wonderful lady.

I was the baby of the family, and my name is Hope. When I was born, my oldest sister was already eighteen years old. From an early age, it was always understood that I would be the caregiver for my parents when the time came. As time progressed, I left home, graduated from college, married, obtained a great job, and was blessed with a beautiful baby girl. Life was great, but a major storm was beginning to unfold that would continue for the next fourteen years.

I started to notice my active, outgoing mother was no longer proactively engaging with people. As time progressed, so did her symptoms. Mom, who was a fabulous cook, stopped cooking. She enjoyed traveling but no longer wanted to leave home for extended trips. She loved to care for people and reach out to those in need; all this stopped. Physical symptoms started to manifest in the form of losing weight, headaches, and a partial loss of vision. Mom clearly had a severe problem, but my father and family were in denial. Everyone made little excuses for Mom and pretended not to notice the changes. It was like a big elephant in the middle of the room, and no one wanted to acknowledge it. The family was in shock.

Within a year, Mom started to wonder away from home. Dad did his best to care for her night and day. He began using local senior resources for adult day care when it was available, but the day to day pressures left him exhausted. One day, while he was busy taking care of household chores, Mom walked out the front door and wandered off in her bathrobe. A friend happened to find her standing outside a local grocery store with her pockets full of kiwi. Mom didn't even like kiwi. She was completely disoriented when I picked her up.

At this point, my husband and I began to discuss and pray about care options for my mother. After weeks of focused prayer, it was clear God was leading me to quit my job to care for my mom. Quitting my job would result in a 46% cut to our annual income. I kept thinking, "Really, a 46% cut – what is God asking us to do?" However, together we trusted God completely – after all, who were we to question God? For the next six months, we lived 100% off my husband's salary to ensure we could cover our monthly bills. Things were tight, but amazingly, our finances worked. So we decided to take a major leap of faith. I quit my job and never looked back. For the next ten years, God took care of us day after day. Miraculously, the finances just took care of themselves. We were blessed over and over. God was faithful as we trusted and followed Him.

My daughter and I began spending the days with Mom and Dad. Mom continued to deteriorate, now unable to dress and handle personal care. I could see her slipping away right in front of me. I prayed every day that God would give me the strength to handle this difficult situation. I tried to keep a positive outlook, but it was hard. We remained busy with trips to the fish hatchery, apple orchards, and simple outings to keep Mom and Dad active. I enjoyed the special time with them, and my little daughter was spending quality, cherished time with her grandparents.

I remember late one night I received a frantic call from my father that Mom had wandered out of the house and he could not locate her anywhere. After several hours of searching, Dad (who was always precise on details) saw a brown Aerostar station wagon pull up, drop her off at their house and simply disappear. Mom was perfectly fine and happy. We later realized the make, model, and color of that car did not exist. How odd. We firmly believe God had an angel bring Mom home that night. We have no other explanation. While the situation was very scary, it reminded me that God was watching over us.

For the next several months, I did my best to care for Mom. Her mind continued to slip away right before my eyes. This strong woman that I adored was disappearing inch by inch, hour by hour, day by day. I was sad. To complicate the situation, Dad's health began to decline rapidly. He was diagnosed with congestive heart failure. I can recall thinking and praying, "God...really? What am I going to do now? Why is this happening?" I continued to do my best to provide loving care for my mother and daughter while being a faithful wife. Did I now need to add my dad to the list? To be honest, I was exhausted and completely drained of energy.

Thank goodness for the good news. I believe in the power of prayer! I knew, based on His promises in the Bible, God would not abandon me. I kept praying for His intervention, and I continued trusting Him. Then one day, the most amazing thing happened. I began to find strength and hope from God through Bible scriptures. The scriptures I had read many times before were coming alive. They were speaking to my heart as they comforted me. It was extremely powerful and humbling. The following Bible verse gave me renewed strength and hope on a daily basis. I read it over and over:

Psalm 116:1-7 (NIV)

I love the Lord, for he heard my voice; he heard my cry for mercy. Because he turned his ear to me, I will call on him as long as I live.

The cords of death entangled me, the anguish of the grave came over me; I was overcome by distress and sorrow. Then I called on the name of the Lord: "Lord, save me!"

The Lord is gracious and righteous; our God is full of compassion. The Lord protects the unwary; when I was brought low, he saved me. Return to your rest, my soul, for the Lord has been good to you.

The weeks continued to pass. Then, one day, my dad sat me down out of the blue and had a very direct conversation with me. I can still recall his words, "Hope, the Lord has been good to me. I want you to know how grateful I am that you are taking such good care of your Mom." Two days later, my Father passed away.

My husband and I continued to pray and ask for guidance after Dad's death. Our small, remote desert town had minimal senior care options, and there were financial limitations we needed to consider. After daily prayer and a family conference, we decided it was best if my five-year-old daughter and I moved in with my mom so I could provide 24/7 care. After several hard months, I could feel myself starting to sink. I was exhausted.

We finally made the difficult decision to transition Mom into a nursing home, where she received loving care for over nine years. I was blessed to continue spending time with her on a daily basis. She did not always know me by name, but I valued and enjoyed the simple things in life with her. Just sitting on her bed and appreciating the opportunity to pray with my mother filled my heart with joy.

While living at the nursing home, Mom continued to touch people's lives through her unwavering love for God. It was amazing to watch her attend the weekly Sunday services held in the small dining hall. While she was now unable to remember most of her life or her children, she never forgot her adoration for God. No matter what happened through her dementia journey, her deep commitment to our Lord never went away. God was her foundation. He was in her heart and soul. Mom would smile and nod her head when old church hymns were played on the piano, even though she could not remember the words or how to sing. She would bow her head and pray, even when confused. Until Mom's last breath, she continued to worship God with her limited abilities that remained.

"Love the Lord your God with all your heart and with all your soul and with all your mind." Matthew 22:37 (NIV)

In closing, it was a blessing and my privilege to be with my mother on her difficult journey. I am so thankful for the time I had with her. I never once questioned God's faithfulness. He was with me the whole way. Praise God!

Hope and her Mom, Mary Lee

REFLECTION

1. Are there some areas in your life where you need or want God's guidance or direction? *Yes / Maybe / No*
   If yes or maybe, take a moment and write those areas down.

_____

_____

_____

_____

_____

_____

_____

_____

_____

2. Are you trying to accomplish things on your own?
   Do you feel exhausted or need help? *Yes / Maybe / No*
   If yes or maybe, what are those things?

_____

_____

_____

_____

_____

_____

_____

_____

_____

3. What is stopping you from asking God for guidance, support, or help on the items you listed in Steps 1 and 2 above? Circle all the things below that describe why you have not asked God for guidance or help:

I'm afraid   *I don't know how to ask God*   *I've made mistakes*

I'm embarrassed   *I'm too busy*   *I'm too tired*

I feel unworthy   *I'm angry*   *I feel overwhelmed*

I forgot to ask God

Other: _____

NEXT STEPS

There is Good News – You are a child of God. He cares about you – including all the issues, concerns, and problems you wrote down above.

Don't let the items you circled in Step 3 stop you from asking God for direction, help, guidance, or support. No matter what is going on in your life right now (or in your past), God stands ready to help you and to provide guidance. All you need to do is ask Him. Yes, it really is that simple.

From caregiver issues to financial matters;
From infidelity issues to abortions;
From drug issues to work issues;
From family issues to anxiety issues;
The list goes on and on….

CLOSING PRAYER

Dear God,

Thank you for caring about me. I need your guidance and direction. Will you please help me with _____? I know that you may not answer my prayer right away, but I also know that you love me and hear me. I will continue to pray and seek your help and guidance. Thank you! Amen.

Losing a Sibling to Suicide

"For God so loved the world that he gave his one and only Son, that whoever believes in him shall not perish but have eternal life. For God did not send his Son into the world to condemn the world, but to save the world through him." John 3:16-17 (NIV)

Laura sobbed as she held Rick's lifeless body in her arms. While she lovingly looked into his handsome face, she softly stroked his hair with her hand. His eyes were now closed, and his face was drawn. It was obvious he had been crying; tears were dried on his cheeks and around his nose. Rick, her wonderful brother, was gone.

Rick's journey began thirty-one years earlier in a small community located in the middle of the Mojave Desert. He was one of six children born into a family that was traumatized for many years by an abusive, alcoholic father. His mother, on the other hand, was an amazing Christian woman who deeply loved her children and the Lord. They were raised in the hope of the Lord, not in the hope of the earth. They knew God would carry them through the storms of life, including the wrath of their earthly father. They valued and embraced their deep need for our Savior, Jesus Christ and the importance of family.

At a young age, Rick had a soft heart for the Lord. He knew he could always depend on God and sought refuge in Him throughout his life. Based on his upbringing, Rick tried to mirror Jesus by caring for people less fortunate than himself and looking out for the underdogs that always seemed to struggle. Perhaps he identified with these special people because he was an underdog when it came to his father's wrath. When his father exploded into alcoholic rampages, Rick and his brothers received the brunt of his damaging anger. His father's abusive, drunken rages stained Rick's heart, soul, and mind while contributing to his lifelong struggle with depression and low self-esteem.

In elementary and middle school, Rick found a way to make sense of his small world through athletic achievements and being a friend to all. For a while, his strong drive to achieve success through sports made him feel better about himself. As the years progressed, Rick continued to find success and contentment through baseball and football. In high school, he was extremely popular as he continued to excel in athletics. Both his coaches and peers admired him. He was committed to teamwork and dedicated to a strong work ethic, values he learned from his family—especially his mother and grandparents.

Despite his popularity and success, Rick quietly struggled. He wrestled with the clash of two different worlds. His external world was full of accolades, recognition, and praise for his athletic accomplishments. However, Rick's private world was somber, insecure, and uncomfortable. He lacked self-confidence and felt he was unworthy.

Before his junior year in high school, he had a serious conversation with his mother. A discussion you would not typically associate with a teenage boy. He shared how he felt unworthy of the recognition he received and the success he had experienced. He felt guilty that many good, but less fortunate people did not have the same opportunities he had been afforded. Therefore, as a way to stand-up for those less fortunate, Rick decided to not participate in varsity football his junior year.

His desire to reach out to underprivileged people was heartfelt and genuine. He was compelled to protect those who were not considered "good enough" for popularity or accolades. Unfortunately, in his passion and quest to help people, he soon opened a dangerous door. He began to associate with a group of students who were mixed-up in alcohol and drugs. As he tried to cope with his internal struggles, he began to party with his new friends. Rick started to use alcohol as a way to "fit in," while numbing his internal conflicts with minimal consequences. Before long, he was the athletic student star who was also best buddies with the party gang. As his partying intensified, he was soon pulled into a darker side of the world where he began to experience alcohol abuse, much like his father.

After graduation, Rick attended a community college where he successfully played baseball and continued to have a very active social life. Partying became a regular part of his evenings and weekends which impacted his studies. Unfortunately, due to his hereditary disposition, he soon found himself entrapped in an alcohol addiction just like his father. As time progressed, he began to experiment with drugs, despite warnings from his mother and siblings. Laura shared, "Satan knew Rick's weaknesses, and he attacked with a vengeance." He did not graduate from college and soon accepted a construction job to pay his bills and support his lifestyle.

While living a very risky lifestyle, he met a woman who also enjoyed the party scene. At age twenty-five, Rick proposed and they were married. He viewed marriage as a lifelong commitment and took his vows seriously. However, from the beginning, their marriage was on shaky ground due to their addictions. Two years after their marriage, they were blessed with a healthy little boy. Rick was thrilled and determined to be the father he always longed for as he tried to straighten out his life. He wanted to be successful in God's eyes and his son's.

Unfortunately, their marriage suffered as their dysfunctional lifestyles continued and their incompatibilities magnified. Despite Rick's attempts to fight for their marriage, his wife decided to leave with their son. She filed for divorce after three years of marriage, ignoring his desperate pleas to keep their family together. He was devastated and viewed the divorce as a personal failure. Rick was hard on himself and never completely recovered from his failed marriage.

After the divorce, he strived to be an involved father and spent quality time with his son whenever possible. Despite his alcohol addiction, he was propelled by a loving heart and did his best to be a devoted dad, son, brother, and friend. Rick continued to have a deep love for the Lord, but he could not get his life together. He attended church with Laura and would weep as he sat in the church pew. He was caught in a vicious cycle of depression, substance abuse, and low self-esteem; he felt trapped, ashamed, and unworthy. Rick was vulnerable to Satan's ugly whispers due to the alcohol and drugs that haunted him.

After a few years, Rick entered into another relationship. This time, he was blessed with a precious baby girl. The joy of his little girl lifted his spirits and carried him for a few months. He was a proud father but soon became disillusioned and bewildered once again as regular employment in the construction field eluded him. He passionately wanted to be a positive role model for his children as he strived to provide for his family. Unfortunately, financial challenges continued to mount, his current relationship began to fracture, and the separation from his son weighed heavily on his heart. Soon, a sense of worthlessness clouded his thinking as his depression deepened and alcoholism became a way of life.

Then around Christmas in 1988, Rick lost another job and struggled to make ends meet. Although it was difficult and embarrassing, he asked to borrow money from family members to start a new business. Despite the fact that times were tough, he was determined to be a man of his word, pay back the money, and turn his life around. Then, in January of 1989, his life became very dark. He found himself in the pit of despair, and he felt hopeless.

He was emotionally distraught and lost touch with reality as he continued to drink, and his depression intensified.

Two nights before his death, Rick called his oldest sister, who lived several hours away. They talked for a long time as she listened intently. Pam did her best to be empathetic to his feelings and concerns. He was in despair and was drinking as he shared his struggles and disappointments. Before they finally said good night, she told her brother that she loved him. He seemed better, at least for the moment.

The next night, he called his little sister Laura, who lived about an hour away. They also talked at length as he shared his disappointments. He was discouraged about his unemployment and lack of success with his new business. Rick was ashamed of his failures and was brokenhearted. He believed he was unworthy of love and goodness. Laura did her best to encourage Rick and reminded him to be nice to himself. Before they hung up, she said "I love you" and promised to come visit him the next day.

Laura was up early the following morning and took care of some business on her way to see her brother. The brisk winter day was going well until she received an alarming call. Rick's girlfriend sobbed as she told Laura to go to Rick's house immediately. Upon arriving, she saw several police cars parked in front of his house, and she panicked. As Laura ran to the front door, his girlfriend broke the heart-wrenching news. Rick committed suicide. He hung himself in the garage.

Laura was in shock as she rushed to the hospital. The experience of entering the hospital morgue and seeing Rick's lifeless body was horrible. She sobbed hysterically as she carefully held him in her arms and called him brother, but there was no response. He was gone.

The next week was a blur as Rick's brothers and sisters surrounded their broken mother with the love and compassion she showed them throughout their lives. The entire family was devastated and overwhelmed by grief as they reached out to God for comfort. They knew God was the only way they would survive this insurmountable pain; pain that was intertwined with questions and confusion. Their emotional shock and collective guilt that they missed opportunities to help Rick was openly discussed. Furthermore, their hearts were heavily burdened for Rick's children, as they knew the impact of this event would adversely influence their lives forever. The loss was too great for words. They cried together.

The church had standing room only, as over 400 friends gathered at a memorial service to pay their respect to Rick and his grieving family. He was loved and admired by many people. As the day progressed, his family found comfort in the positive stories and kind words that were offered and shared. For a moment in time, it broke the chains of despair and allowed everyone to remember the happier times. God was with them throughout the day as He surrounded the entire family with peace and compassion. As a result of Rick's love for God and others, his family selected words from 2 John 1:5 for his headstone, "Love God, Love One Another." It was the way he wanted to live his life.

Due to the way Rick died, some people did not know what to say or how to act around the family. Sometimes a social stigma or cloud can surround suicide survivors, leaving the family isolated. However, the family chose to take comfort in the awkward smiles, warm notes, and heartfelt hugs that people offered. They valued the presence of people that loved Rick, even if they were unable to find the words to express their feelings. They treasured their kindness and love.

The following week was extremely emotional as the family continued to grieve. Their mother's house was dark and very quiet. It was different. It was now time for her children to step up and take charge, the way she had so many times when they were frightened by their father. As the family sat together day and night, they continued their painful journey of openly sharing how they felt about Rick's suicide. They talked about their guilt and anger as they gained comfort by pouring out their sadness and confusion. Together, they did their best to openly grieve and pray for God's comfort, guidance, and peace. They were extremely thankful for the small community of loving friends that gathered with them, listened, and prayed.

The time came for family members to journey home as their grieving process transcended to a different level. As Rick's sister Pam began her long drive home, the sky was dark and overcast. As she traveled across long stretches of desert, Pam started to cry and pour her heart out to God, "Please, please give me a sign that my brother is OK. I need to know he is with you." Suddenly, an amazing event occurred that took her breath away. The clouds unexpectedly parted for only a few seconds, as a stunning ray of sunlight vibrantly beamed right in front of her car. Then, an incredible thing happened, "I felt God's power, warmth, and comfort wash over me as an intense tingling started at the top of my head, traveled through my body and out my feet. I was instantly covered in total serenity and peace. Then, the clouds closed just as quickly as they had opened. I drove home in complete peace. God heard my pleas and answered my prayers that day. I will forever be thankful."

Romans 8:35-39 (NIV)

Who shall separate us from the love of Christ? Shall trouble or hardship or persecution or famine or nakedness or danger or sword? As it is written: "For your sake we face death all day long; we are considered as sheep to be slaughtered." No, in all these things we are more than conquerors through him who loved us. For I am convinced that neither death nor life, neither angels nor demons, neither the present nor the future, nor any powers, neither height nor depth, nor anything else in all creation, will be able to separate us from the love of God that is in Christ Jesus our Lord.

God knew Rick's heart on that lonely afternoon when he took his last breath. He was sick. He suffered from severe depression and lost hope. Rick was emotionally distraught and lost his moral compass, which left him unable to judge right from wrong. Thankfully, our all-loving God is just, merciful, and forgiving. He provides the gift of atonement for the salvation of people who are incapable of moral responsibility or too young to understand. For those who are capable of distinguishing right from wrong, He offers them "free will" with the gift to confess their sins, repent, and believe in Jesus.

Romans 3:25-26 (NIV)

God presented Christ as a sacrifice of atonement, through the shedding of his blood—to be received by faith. He did this to demonstrate his righteousness, because in his forbearance he had left the sins committed beforehand unpunished— he did it to demonstrate his righteousness at the present time, so as to be just and the one who justifies those who have faith in Jesus.

Laura and her family firmly believe Rick was not morally responsible for his actions that day. He confessed his love for God throughout his life and believed Jesus was his personal Savior, even when his depression led him down an unhealthy path. Laura shared, "I know our Lord is full of love, compassion, and mercy. He knew my brother was broken and under the attack of Satan. I firmly believe Jesus embraced Rick in His arms that day and healed his broken heart. I don't know why he suffered the way he did, but we are grateful for our Lord who loves us unconditionally."

Many years have now passed since Rick's death. His brothers and sisters have healed in different ways as they continue to support each other. God has been with each one of them through their healing journey. Through their questions, guilt, anger, and sadness, He has never abandoned them. Rick's siblings believe part of their purpose here on earth is to serve others who are dealing with pain and suicides. An important part of their recovery has been nurturing their relationship with Rick's children and loving them. They are grateful for the time they had with Rick here on earth and look forward to seeing him in heaven. There is hope in our fallen world, and His name is Jesus!

Psalm 103:1-6 (NIV)

Praise the Lord, my soul;
all my inmost being, praise his holy name.
Praise the Lord, my soul,
and forget not all his benefits—
who forgives all your sins
and heals all your diseases,
who redeems your life from the pit
and crowns you with love and compassion,
who satisfies your desires with good things
so that your youth is renewed like the eagle's.

The Lord works righteousness
and justice for all the oppressed.

REFLECTION

1. Do you know someone who is severely depressed and feeling hopeless? Are you worried they might harm themselves or try to commit suicide? Don't ignore your concerns or minimize their feelings. Reach out to them and listen with compassion. Pray with them and for them. Below are some suggested resources that can help:

    - Your local police department—dial 911 if it is an emergency

    - National Suicide Lifeline *1-800-273-8255* *http://suicidepreventionlifeline.org*

    - Your local hospital

    - Employee assistance hotline

    - Your minister, pastor, or priest

    - Family members or close friends

2. Moving forward as a survivor of a loved one who committed suicide is difficult, but there is hope. God deeply cares about your pain and heartaches. You are never alone on your earthly journey. There are a variety of resources available to help you. Do not be afraid or ashamed to ask for help.

    - Reach out to God and pray. He already knows your heartaches. Ask Him to heal your emotional wounds. If you feel you missed signs that your friend or loved one was in trouble, release that burden to God and forgive yourself with His help. Lean on Him for strength and peace as you move forward.

    - Openly share your feelings with family and friends. Ask them to pray for you.

    - Talk with your pastor, minister, or priest about your feelings

    - Join a suicide support group

    - Seek professional counseling if you find yourself unable to move forward.

3. When someone dies as a result of suicide, guilt, shock, and confusion can complicate the grieving process. Grieving and healing for survivors can be a lonely journey. Sometimes, due to the social

stigma associated with suicide, people avoid the grieving family because the situation is uncomfortable. They are unsure of what to say or what to do.

Do you know someone who survived the suicide of a friend or family member? *Yes / No*

If yes, it is important that grieving suicide survivors are not ignored. They are suffering through the loss of a loved one – period! They need people to be with them on their healing journey. Don't be afraid. How would God have you help and support them?

_____

_____

_____

_____

NEXT STEPS

1. As we saw in Rick's story, Satan will use whatever he can to destroy us. If you open the door to risky behaviors or habits, the adversary will seize on that opportunity and attack you.

   Pause and reflect.

   • Are you involved with dangerous habits, behaviors, or activities?

   • Are you doing things that you do not want your family or friends to know about?

   • Are you involved with things that are not acceptable in the Lord's eyes?

   _____

   _____

   _____

   _____

   Do you want to stop? *Yes / No*

If you answered yes, confess your actions to God today by praying this simple prayer:

Dear God,

I am involved with _____ and I know it is unacceptable to you. Please forgive me. Help me to stop and turn away from this behavior. Please guide and support me as I move forward. Amen.

2. Congratulations on taking the first step to turn your life around. Reach out to someone today (a pastor, friend, counselor, support group) and ask them to help you as you move forward. You may be facing some hard work as you turn your life around. Don't despair. Allow people to help you as God strengthens and guides you.

CLOSING PRAYER

Dear God,

Please keep my eyes and ears open to notice people who are hurting and need help. Help me to support those who are grieving a loss, regardless of the situation. Please give me a heart of love, compassion, and awareness. Thank you. Amen.

Living with Chronic Pain

"My comfort in my suffering is this: Your promise preserves my life." Psalm 119:50 (NIV)

Nathalie was exhausted as she slowly opened the front door to escape the snowy, blustery Virginia night. As she stepped into her warm home, she could barely move due to the cramping and aching throughout her body. The chronic pain was attacking with rage, and it was not retreating. She slowly removed her favorite black hat and attempted to remove her furry winter coat. Then, without notice, the cramping in her hands intensified. It made it impossible to unbutton her coat, so she stopped. When she gradually made her way into the kitchen to brew some hot tea, she endured sharp, deep stabbing pains in her legs making it extremely difficult to walk. As she carefully pulled out a chair at the kitchen table to finally catch her breath, the excruciating pain in her hips and back made it nearly unbearable to sit. Nathalie was experiencing the effects of living with fibromyalgia.

Nathalie's pain and parallel faith journey started as a small child. From an early age, Nathalie was plagued with pain. Despite her agony, she always knew God was with her and loved her. At age ten, she was infected with chicken pox and rheumatic fever at the same time. She was extremely ill and was never physically the same after the combined illness. At first, the family doctor attributed her symptoms to growing pains and prescribed aspirin. However, as the pain persisted it also intensified. Then, she began to experience other odd symptoms such as impaired vision and hearing. At age twelve, she was diagnosed with juvenile arthritis, the same year she accepted Jesus into her heart. From that point forward, she made the brave and mature decision not to let her illness define her. She placed her faith in God, gained her strength from Him on a daily basis, and powered through her illness.

During her teenage years, Nathalie strived not to identify herself or her limitations with juvenile arthritis. She did not want attention or sympathy. Due to financial constraints, her family was unable to pursue medical specialists to address her physical issues. So, she decided to surrender her illness to God and depended on Him for strength. She gained great comfort from the following Bible verse:

"My grace is sufficient for you, for my power is made perfect in weakness." 2 Corinthians 12:9 (NIV)

While her high school journey was plagued with chronic pain, the energy of her youth helped balance her physical challenges. She refused to use her illness as an excuse. Through pure determination and her trust in God, Nathalie managed to actively and successfully participate in a variety of sports including basketball, softball, and track. However, when she exerted herself during practices, games, or track events, intense pain always followed. It was through this daily pain that she learned a valuable lesson that made her wise beyond her years. Nathalie learned how to "power through" the difficult, painful times in her life by surrendering her weaknesses to God and leaning on Him for strength. She understood that life, love, and strength come directly from God and she was grateful. In retrospect, her physical challenges, despite the pain, actually prepared Nathalie for the life that God had planned for her. Through her pain, her eyes were opened to those that were less fortunate. She developed a heart of compassion for the brokenhearted and wanted to make a difference.

The years went on, and so did Nathalie's chronic pain and fatigue. There were days when the pain was so intense that the mere act of brushing her teeth or combing her hair was nearly impossible. Despite her physical limitations, she continued to serve the Lord and joyfully help others. She became actively involved with outreach. She led children's church and supported missionary work in her local town including visits to nursing homes and raking leaves for the elderly. Nathalie kept an open heart and strived to help hurting and lonely people. She would willingly go any place where she could make someone's life better while sharing the good news about God's love and promises.

Then one day, the pain was extremely intense, and the symptoms were so severe, her family feared she had a stroke. After running several tests, the doctors determined she now had fibromyalgia. Despite the depressing diagnosis, she was determined to fight on and not let the illness define her, a pattern she established earlier in life. She knew Satan wanted her to be self-absorbed by her physical weaknesses. He wanted her to believe she was no longer able to fulfill God's purpose for her life. It was at this point, Nathalie asked the Lord to heal her body if it was His will, but she never asked why she had the illness. She boldly prayed the following prayer:

> *"Dear Lord,*
> *My body and mind are weak. I know you have*
> *a purpose for my life. I lay down my physical*
> *weaknesses before you. I ask that you spiritually*
> *strengthen me so I may accomplish your will. Amen."*

Since that time, God has continued to be faithful to Nathalie, and she has continued to be faithful to God. While her physical issues continue and she has not been healed, she has found joy in an amazing life being spiritually strong in the Lord. She knows her illness keeps her humble and she willingly depends on God. Nathalie has learned to rest and lean on God for her strength every day. He has shown her grace on her hardest days when her body just will not cooperate. On those exhaustingly, painful days, she prays this simple prayer:

> *"Father, please lift me up and help me to move*
> *forward in your strength. I am tired, worn-out, and*
> *weak. Strengthen me to do your work today. Amen."*

Interestingly, she discovered that on her toughest days, God uses her most effectively. When she has been unable to walk, she has felt the Lord lead her to pick up the phone and call specific people that she has not interacted with for months. On two separate occasions, she was stunned to discover her phone calls interrupted individuals contemplating suicide. She knows this was not a coincidence, but all part of God's plan for her life.

Nathalie understands and embraces the fact that God has a purpose for her life way beyond her pain. Due to her compassion for brokenhearted people, she has been honored to share her personal story and God's promises with numerous women; women who have gone through challenges and pain in their lives including abuse, divorce, abandonment, abortions, cancer, illiteracy, and low self-esteem. She has compassionately helped them identify and surrender their pain and heartaches to God through prayer. Nathalie has celebrated with them as they laid down their burdens and accepted God's promises. It has given her great joy to see these women move forward with their lives, holding their heads high, thanks to the grace of God. The following Bible verse inspired her as she searched for the brokenhearted:

"The Spirit of the Sovereign Lord is on me, because the Lord has anointed me to proclaim good news to the poor. He has sent me to bind up the brokenhearted, to proclaim freedom for the captives and release from darkness for the prisoners." Isaiah 61:1 (NIV)

Nathalie has recently started a non-profit organization called Jacobs Well. It is a mobile outreach movement that provides nutritional needs and emergency services to hurting people in the Washington D.C. area. God continues to use Nathalie's life and story. She is determined to live way beyond the pain as she lives in His promises and fulfills His purpose for her life.

REFLECTION

1. God has a purpose for all our lives if we are willing to follow and trust Him. Have you asked God what His purpose is for your life? *Yes / No*

   If you answered yes, are you fulling His purpose for your life? Write down the thoughts that come into your mind.

   If you have not asked God what His purpose is for your life, you can pray the simple prayer below, then be still and listen. Write down what comes to your mind.

   Dear God, I want to be faithful to your will. What is your purpose for my life?

   _____

   _____

   _____

   _____

   _____

   _____

   _____

   _____

   _____

   _____

   _____

   _____

   _____

   _____

   _____

NEXT STEPS

1. Ask God what next steps you should take to fulfill His purpose for your life. In the space below, write down what comes into your mind. Add a date if you are willing to start working on the action(s).

ACTION	START

2. As you reflect on Nathalie's story, do you have a physical or emotional pain you want to turn over to God? If yes, pray this simple prayer:

   Dear God,

   I have been living with pain, and I need your help. I am tired and can no longer move forward alone. I am turning _____ over to you. Please free me from this burden and strengthen me spiritually as I move forward with my life. Thank you. Amen.

CLOSING PRAYER

Dear God,

Thank you for meeting me right where I am as I look forward, not backward. Please help me to fulfill YOUR purpose and plans for my life. Thank you for your guidance, direction, strength, and unconditional love. Amen.

Moving Through Betrayal

The doorbell rang. As Ellen slowly opened the front door, a stranger was standing there. He looked her straight in the eye and kindly said, "Are you Ellen?" In a questioning tone, she said, "Yes." He continued, "Is your husband George?" She hesitantly replied, "Yes." "Do you have any idea where your husband is right now?" Her heart began to pound as she said, "I don't know." Then the man replied, "He is having dinner with my wife. I've been tracking the two of them for months. They both know I'm here to inform you about their relationship." Ellen was stunned.

Ellen grew up as an only child in a conservative, loving Christian home. She adored her parents and was proud of her father, who was also the pastor at her church. She was a good kid and carefully adhered to her Christian beliefs. Ellen focused on doing the right things in life and always followed the rules.

After graduating from high school, she attended a Christian College where she quickly made wonderful friends. George attended the same college, and they started to date. Like Ellen, he was also an only child and grew up in a Christian home with parents who were very involved with their church. On paper, he met all her criteria for a potential husband. They seemed to be the "perfect pair," and she quickly fell "head over heels" in love. However, her friends were quite concerned. George did not have a good reputation on campus. Ellen seemed happy, so her friends accepted their relationship and did not say anything. Unfortunately, George slowly pulled her away from her friends so he could be the center of her attention.

For the next four years, Ellen was blind when it came to George. She ignored red flag after red flag regarding their relationship. George regularly made her feel uncomfortable due to his relentless flirting with other women. His flirting made her feel insecure and fearful that she was not good enough. Deep down she sensed her concerns and had trust issues, but chose to disregard her feelings. Ellen and George also argued on a regular basis. However, she was in love and did not want to admit their relationship had major issues. She continued to overlook the "elephant in the room" and moved forward. In the middle of her senior year, they were engaged, and wedding plans commenced.

In the spring following their college graduation, Ellen enjoyed her dream wedding complete with her father officiating the ceremony. As they began to sail through years of marriage, the unaddressed issues from their years of dating continued to haunt them. From the outside, their marriage appeared to be wonderful, almost perfect, as they pursued professional careers and became involved with their local church. However, behind closed doors, their arguing continued to escalate, incompatibility problems persisted, and trust issues remained.

Then, in the spring of 1999, the day before their twelfth wedding anniversary, they had an explosive argument regarding dinner plans to celebrate their anniversary. However, on this particular day and during this specific argument, Ellen could sense something had drastically changed. George was different. She immediately felt something was seriously wrong and she knew their marriage was in trouble.

Their anniversary fell on a Sunday. George chose not to attend church for the first time in their marriage. He also shut down all communication with her. Ellen was extremely concerned and overwhelmed by the situation, so she decided to reach out to her parents who lived over 500 miles away. They began to pray as Ellen buckled down for a personal storm she never saw coming.

For the next month, George was cold as ice and refused to engage in conversations. He moved into their guest bedroom and began arriving home around midnight on a regular basis. On weekends, he would simply disappear with no explanation. He stopped attending church. On the other hand, Ellen was an emotional wreck and in a state of confusion. She sought guidance from her pastor as she leaned on her parents and friends for support and prayer. Ellen also reached out to George's parents and shared the challenges they were experiencing. She asked them to pray.

As the days passed, the deafening silence continued as Ellen tried to give George space to mentally work through his situation. She was living on eggshells and unable to relax. Their fractured marriage was consuming her. One night, she found herself lying face down on her bedroom floor sobbing and begging God to fix their marriage, but no immediate answers came. It was quiet.

As Ellen's mind filled with questions, she began reflecting on times in the past when she had fleeting thoughts that George might be involved with someone else. She asked her dad if she should hire a private investigator. He calmly replied, "Ellen, if something is going on, it will come to you. You will not need a private investigator." He reminded her that God does not always answer our prayers the way we want or in the timeframe we desire. He may have a different plan.

Psalm 37:7-8 (NIV)

Be still before the Lord and wait patiently for him; do not fret when people succeed in their ways, when they carry out their wicked schemes. Refrain from anger and turn from wrath; do not fret—it leads only to evil.

As the month of silence came to a close, George suddenly started talking as if nothing was wrong. He informed Ellen he would be leaving early Friday morning to enjoy a long golf weekend on the coast with his friend Robert. As he grabbed his golf clubs and walked out Friday morning, she noticed he was wearing a T-shirt instead of a golf shirt. She thought it was odd and moved on with her morning. Then the phone rang, "Is George there?" Ellen responded to the gentleman, "He's not available right now." And then she heard words that made her sick to her stomach, "This is Robert. Please tell George I'm out on the local golf course. We have a friend in town, so I can't golf with him today."

When the call ended, Ellen became angry. George had crossed the line. He intentionally deceived her. As the day progressed and suspicions mounted, she decided to conduct her own private investigation. When Ellen called their credit card company, she learned George booked a hotel room only forty minutes away and withdrew money from the ATM. He was not on the coast with Robert as he had indicated. Ellen then called his mother and shared the disturbing information. As their phone conversation progressed, they decided to drive to George's office together. They found his parked car with his golf clubs in the back seat. Obviously, he was not golfing. They were both extremely upset. George had lied.

When George arrived home that Sunday evening, both Ellen and his mother confronted him. He was shell-shocked but denied he was having an affair. He admitted he was with another woman. Despite being together in a hotel room charged to George and Ellen's credit card, he claimed they were only friends.

> *"Save me, Lord, from lying lips and from deceitful tongues." Psalm 120:2 (NIV)*

The next three weeks were very tense, and nothing was resolved as they continued to live under the same roof. It was a weird existence as George continued to come and go as he pleased. At the advice of her pastor, Ellen sought the help of a Christian counselor as she tried to process her devastating situation. She began taking some medication to counteract her anxiety. Then out of the blue on a late Saturday afternoon, the husband of George's mistress showed up at Ellen's home, and they began to compare notes. The affair had been going on for months. At that moment, she recalled her father's words six weeks earlier, "If something is going on, it will come to you." She realized God was with her and He was in the driver's seat.

Ellen finally decided to leave their house and remove herself from the painful situation to gain perspective. Her employer granted a leave of absence as Ellen's father flew in to provide support and help her pack. The night before they drove to her parent's house, her father showed remarkable constraint that could only come from God. As George opened the front door and sauntered into the house, he was surprised to see his father-in-law standing with Ellen. As he pretended nothing odd was going on, Ellen looked him straight in the eye and informed him she was leaving in the morning. She later asked her father how he exercised such constraint given the terrible things George had done. He shared, "For my salvation, I knew I had to forgive George. I prayed God would help me forgive him so I could help you."

When Ellen went to bed that night, she was surprised when George came in the bedroom and suddenly wanted to engage in a meaningful conversation after weeks of silence. He asked, "Why are you leaving?" She was appalled he would ask such a question. Before she could say a word, a very odd phenomenon seemed to take over her body. As she looked at George, she was unable to talk. She was powerless to form words or articulate anything verbally. In retrospect, Ellen believes God took control of the situation that night and protected her exhausted, emotional, and fragile heart.

For the next three months, Ellen remained with her parents. There were many dark days when she could barely drag herself out of bed due to her overwhelming sadness. Her parents loved and protected her as she slipped into a state of depression. When she could no longer pray, others prayed for her. There were days of deep soul searching and crying as she desperately tried to figure out her life and next steps. Throughout it all, Ellen tried to be a good person despite the betrayal, lies, and pain. Then one day, she received an upsetting call from the mistress's husband confirming the affair was continuing. He was devastated, and so was Ellen. The emotional roller-coaster left her heartbroken.

A divorce was never a consideration for Ellen based on her Christian upbringing. After all, she was the child of a pastor, what would people think? However, given the situation and the lack of George's remorse for his infidelity, her Christian attorney encouraged her to seriously consider divorce as an option along with her thoughts of reconciliation. Despite her desires, she could not force George to remain in the marriage if he wanted out. In addition, the Bible clearly provides guidance in Matthew 5:32 that it is acceptable to pursue a divorce when adultery has occurred.

During this conflicted time, a family friend who lived through a similar situation sent Ellen a compelling book by James Dobson called Love Must Be Tough. The book provided empowering and proactive "tough love" principles that equipped Ellen with clear guidance for her next steps. The book encouraged her heart and gave her renewed hope as she trusted God to move forward. As the days progressed, God provided clarity on what she was responsible for in the marriage and released her from doubts and the embarrassment surrounding infidelity. It was not her fault.

Ellen decided to be honest with herself and fully transparent by writing a letter to George following the guidance provided in the book. Writing the letter was empowering and provided her with an emotional release and some control over the situation. The letter clearly defined the boundaries for their marriage to move forward including choices George needed to make. She requested his response to the letter within two weeks as she continued to pray for reconciliation. When she finally sent the letter, her parents, pastor, and friends bombarded God with prayers that His will would be done.

One week passed, and there was no reply or phone call from George, only silence. The following week was painful as the days slowly passed. Finally, the two-week deadline was over. George's lack of response or feedback provided her with the peace and confidence she needed. She was grateful her parents sustained her with their prayers and support as she made the hardest decision of her life. After much prayer and soul searching, Ellen filed for divorce. She was at peace with her decision.

> *"Do not be anxious about anything, but in every situation, by prayer and petition, with thanksgiving, present your requests to God." Philippians 4:6 (NIV)*

As Ellen took charge, she demanded that George move out of their house ASAP and she moved back home. He decided to move in with his parents, knowing they were very disappointed in him. Due to their relentless pushing, he finally agreed to pursue marriage counseling. Ellen wanted to ensure she did everything possible to save their marriage, so she agreed. Unfortunately, after a few sessions, it was clear that George was simply going through the motions and unwilling to take accountability for his actions.

There were some efforts to date each other in the following months, but George refused to stop seeing the other woman. In fact, he rebuffed the severity of his actions, often indicating that Ellen was simply over-reacting to their friendship. His unwillingness to tell the truth disturbed her deeply. How could she ever trust him?

As she faced this final crossroad, she again sought the wise counsel of her dad, and he shared the following, "Ellen, do you really want to live the rest of your life like this? If you reconcile with George, what is going to happen the first time he is late - and the second time? You will always have doubts. What will your existence be like?" His comments woke Ellen up, and she proceeded with the divorce. The divorce was finalized during the summer of 2001, and George married his mistress nine months later in the spring of 2002.

While George seamlessly moved forward with his life, Ellen found herself entangled in the aftermath of anger, pain, bitterness and a desire for revenge. She wanted the world to know what the "new happily married couple" had done to her life. The resentment in her heart began to devour her thought process. In reality, the anger was only hurting one person, and that was herself, but she was stuck. Ellen knew forgiveness was the next step she needed to take, but the thought of forgiveness was overwhelming. It was going to take a miracle.

Ellen tried several times to forgive George and his wife, but it was extremely difficult. Every time she thought she forgave them, something would happen, and the painful, angry feelings would come rushing back. It was a vicious circle. Finally, she began to take the process of forgiveness one day at a time. She acknowledged that she was a "work in progress" and unable to forgive them under her own power. She asked God every day to provide the strength and grace she needed to forgive them. After months and months of prayer, she was able to release the entire, messy situation and give it to God. She forgave them and was free of the horrible, heavy burdens she had carried for the past two years. Yes, she still remembered the pain and the events that happened, but they no longer controlled her. God's peace and love replaced the hole in Ellen's broken heart, and she was healed.

"Ask and it will be given to you; seek and you will find; knock and the door will be opened to you." Matthew 7:7 (NIV)

Ellen's story did not end here. An unexpected turn of events, yet again, changed her life forever. With the support of family and friends, she garnered enough courage to explore dating. This was a big step for Ellen, and she was petrified as she prayed for God's help once again. Through a series of incidents that were miracles in themselves, she met a wonderful man named Pete via an on-line dating service. Surprisingly, they were a 100% match, something that rarely occurs. After several emails back and forth, they finally exchanged phone numbers. As they began to "date" via the phone, Pete and Ellen were amazed to discover many similarities in their family histories and the ease in which they communicated. After a month had passed, they decided to meet face-to-face for a casual lunch, and their relationship clicked.

As the months progressed, they fell in love and were married. Pete was the only man she dated after the divorce. Ellen realized he was a gift from God and their chance meeting was not a coincidence. Pete treats her with respect, dignity, and admiration that makes her feel loved, valued, and safe. Their relationship is built on the cornerstone of God's promises and their trust in each other. Together they are fulfilling His purpose for their lives.

In closing, Ellen shared, "God is in the business of restoration. When you think all your hopes are crushed, He can make something beautiful out of your disaster. He will heal your broken heart, but you must learn to be open and trust Him completely, even when you cannot see what lies ahead."

She then added, "Forgiveness was extremely hard for me, but I am so thankful I finally released my heartaches to God. I'm grateful He put the pieces of my life back together and gave me the gift of Pete. I am happier than I ever thought possible. God can and will provide everything your heart needs. He has a purpose for my life, and He has a purpose for yours!" Amen.

REFLECTION

1. Betrayal can come in all sizes and shapes such as lies, stealing, backstabbing, broken promises, secrets, addictions, and infidelity. The effects of betrayal can leave people heartbroken, angry, disillusioned, and emotionally scarred. Pause and reflect for a moment.

   Have you been betrayed? *Yes / No*

   If you answered yes, what did it feel like?

   _____

   _____

   _____

   _____

   _____

   _____

   _____

   _____

2. Are you still carrying the burden of that pain, anger, and heart-break? *Yes / No*

   If you answered yes, who is benefiting from the burden you are carrying?

   _____

   _____

   _____

   _____

   _____

   _____

   _____

   _____

NEXT STEPS

1. Are you ready to let go of your pain, anger, and heartbreak(s)? *Yes / No*

   If yes, list the specific anger, pain, and heartbreak(s) you want to leave behind.

   _____

   _____

   _____

   _____

   _____

   _____

   _____

   _____

CLOSING PRAYER

There is good news! God can help you overcome the scars of betrayal and pain. Begin by praying this simple prayer:

Dear God,

Thank you for loving me unconditionally. I was deeply hurt when _____ resulting in _____. Today, I am releasing this betrayal and turning it over to you. Please remove this heavy burden and pain from my heart and mind. Help me to forgive _____ as I continue to depend on you for my strength and healing. Thank you for helping me. I love you. Amen.

Going Blind

*"Have I not commanded you? Be strong and courageous.
Do not be afraid; do not be discouraged, for the Lord your
God will be with you wherever you go." Joshua 1:9 (NIV)*

The excitement was growing. The months and months of planning and preparation were now complete. As the traditional piano music began to play, the numerous conversations filling the church quieted to whispers. And then, the long-anticipated "Wedding March" started to reverberate throughout the church. As Bessie stood in honor of her daughter walking down the aisle, she strained to catch just one glimpse of Janet as she made her way to the altar. And then, it happened. She captured a slight flicker of blue, yellow, and white as Janet gracefully walked by. While she was unable to see Janet's face, dress, or flowers, her heart was filled with gratitude for the glimpse she was afforded. Within months, Bessie was totally blind.

From an early age, Bessie learned to live with adversity. At age six, her mother died when a doctor accidentally administered a lethal dose of insulin. She was devastated. Her father, with assistance from family members, did his best to raise Bessie and her little sister while juggling the daily demands of their farm. Unfortunately, a few years later, another tragic accident struck. While playing at school, her little sister was kicked in the stomach and died due to complications. It was at this sad time, Bessie's Aunt Beatress (her mother's sister) came to live with them for a short period to provide assistance with cooking and household chores. Together with her father, they did their best to provide a stable, yet strict Christian home environment for Bessie during a very difficult time in her life. They surrounded her with love, and she felt safe.

As time passed, her father and aunt fell in love and were married. Strong Christian values continued to be the foundation of their home as they had children together. Bessie was thrilled. She loved her devoted aunt like a mother, and she was thankful. It was during this time Bessie learned to play the piano and could play many church hymns without the need of music. She loved worshiping the Lord. It gave her great joy.

After graduating from high school, Bessie met her best friend and future husband Channing while attending Pasadena College. They had four wonderful children they raised in a loving, yet strict Christian home, similar to the upbringing she enjoyed. Soon after one of her pregnancies, Bessie was diagnosed with diabetes. The disease and its complications plagued her for the rest of her life. Despite her constant health challenges, she was an involved and engaged mother, and her children adored her.

As time passed, she began to experience eye hemorrhages as a direct result of her diabetes. Each hemorrhage resulted in additional damage to her eyes. She was soon diagnosed with an advanced form of diabetic retinopathy which can lead to blindness when not treated. Bessie's doctors attempted surgery on one eye to correct some of the damage, but the surgery failed. Her situation was far worse than the doctors anticipated. Due to her advanced eye condition, no other operations were attempted, and no other treatments were available at the time. Bessie's eyesight continued to rapidly deteriorate until she was totally blind by age fifty.

It was at this point Bessie made a bold decision. She knew God still had a purpose for her life despite her blindness. Therefore, she decisively chose to continue to seek God's "vision" for her life with a joyful heart instead of living a life filled with anger, discouragement, and self-pity. She chose to follow God's word:

*"The fruit of the Spirit is love, joy, peace,
forbearance, kindness, goodness, faithfulness,
gentleness and self-control." Galatians 5:22-23 (NIV)*

For the next thirty-four years, together with God and her devoted husband, she moved forward on her new journey. God faithfully gave her peace and sustained her as she adapted to a different way of life.

Creativity became a cornerstone in their home. Her goal was to function as independently as possible. Since her husband Channing was still working, Bessie required the ability to safely move around her home and handle daily chores without assistance. Channing, an engineer by trade, installed ropes from room to room to guide Bessie throughout the home while providing stability to prevent a fall. The kitchen ropes guided her to the sink and stove, so she was able to wash dishes and handle basic cooking such as browning meat. He placed raised dots on the kitchen timer, so she was able to time her cooking on the stove and dishes in the oven. The independence and her contributions around the home empowered her and gave her a sense of accomplishment.

God was in every aspect of Bessie's life. She was a strong Christian woman, and God leveraged her faithfulness to help others in need. She was always kind, upbeat, and enjoyed sharing words of encouragement. After her blindness had become a reality, she discovered an amazing outreach via her "Lazy Boy Ministry." For you see, Bessie was not blind on the phone. From her Lazy Boy chair, she handled several calls a week from ladies in the church that wanted to discuss challenges in their lives and explore building a stronger relationship with the Lord. Bessie was honored to patiently and intently listen to their concerns, hardships, and problems. She would offer Bible verses from memory, words of encouragement, and the willingness to pray with them on the phone. It was as if she became an ambassador for God just when people needed a patient ear and some Christian advice.

Of course, Bessie yearned to see her husband, children, and grandchildren, but she was extremely grateful for the visual memories that were lodged in her mind and the joyful sound of their voices. While she lost her ability to read and write, she learned to enjoy books on tape from the Braille Institute and the times that Channing would read passages from the Bible. Bessie missed her ability to see clothes when shopping with her daughters, but she used her sense of touch to feel the soft fabric, pretty buttons, and lace surrounding a collar. Even though she could no longer read music, Bessie enjoyed playing the piano and singing old hymns from her memory. While she could no longer enjoy the beautiful color of a flower, she treasured the feel of its soft petals and fragrant smell.

Bessie was thankful for the simple things in life such as a hug, her husband holding her hand, or the soft kiss of a grandchild. She graciously and courageously learned to leverage her other senses and incredible memory that God had provided. But most of all, Bessie praised God for the many blessings in her life, the gift of salvation through Jesus Christ, and the full life she enjoyed.

REFLECTION

1. We all face different types of challenges throughout our lives. Some problems alter our lives such as Bessie's blindness, some result in financial devastation, while others are annoyances that we sometimes magnify in our minds.

   Pause and reflect on your life. What major adversities, problems, and challenges are you currently facing?

   - _____
   - _____
   - _____
   - _____
   - _____
   - _____

   What minor problems and challenges are distracting you from being "present" in life?

   - _____
   - _____
   - _____
   - _____
   - _____
   - _____

2. Do you have positive things in your life that you are thankful for? If yes, list them below.

   - _____
   - _____
   - _____
   - _____
   - _____

NEXT STEPS

There is good news! No matter what challenges you are facing, God will guide you through life's major and minor storms—if you let Him. Yes, it is your choice.

1. Through God's gift of "free will," you are empowered to choose your response to the problems and challenges in your life. You have two options:

    *   <u>Option A</u>

        You can become paralyzed in your adversity by choosing to be self-absorbed in anger, resentment, revenge, fear, anxiety, embarrassment, and discouragement.

    *   <u>Option B</u>

        You can look up to God for strength and guidance as you maneuver through your challenges. Praise and thank God for the good things in your life, then choose joy and gratitude as you pursue your course of action. Even during critical illnesses and death, God will provide love, peace, gratitude, and compassion to help you through your journey—if you simply open your heart and let Him in.

2. Based on the adversities, problems, and challenges that you identified in the Reflection Section, what positive things will happen in your life if you choose Option A?

_____

_____

_____

_____

_____

_____

_____

_____

3. What positive things could happen if you select Option B?

    _____

    _____

    _____

    _____

    _____

    _____

    _____

4. Through "free will" - it is your choice. Do you want to tackle your adversities, problems, and challenges alone or do you want the guidance and support of God in your life?

    If you are not ready to ask God for help, remember He is available 24/7. He is only a prayer away and loves you unconditionally. If you would like to have God's word at your fingertips, you can access a free on-line Bible at:

    https://www.biblegateway.com/versions/New-International-Version-NIV-Bible

CLOSING PRAYER

If you chose to seek the guidance and support of God, you can immediately reach out to Him through this simple prayer:

Dear God,

Thank you for the blessing in my life. I can no longer tackle my adversities, challenges, and problems on my own. Will you please help me? I am not perfect. Please search my heart and forgive me for the errors that I have made. Please cleanse my heart and help me to seek your guidance and support. Thank you in advance for loving me. Amen.

Tackling Life as a Single Mom

"I have told you these things, so that in me you may have peace. In this world you will have trouble. But take heart! I have overcome the world." John 16:33 (NIV)

Emily trembled as her husband launched into a fit of rage. "Oh, please, not again" she whispered, as fear radiated throughout her body. She quickly moved the children into their rooms for protection, and then braced herself for another night of emotional abuse intensified by his use of alcohol. "What have I done wrong this time?" she thought, as she quickly ran through the day's events. She strived to be the perfect wife, the perfect cook, the perfect mother, but she was never good enough. While her husband never physically hit her, the emotional scars from his verbal abuse and threats left deep wounds that penetrated her soul. What was she going to do?

Emily's story began several years earlier. She was raised in a Christian home and faith was the cornerstone of her values. By age nineteen, she was a beautiful, confident and energetic young woman attending a prestigious university. To help offset college expenses, she accepted an exciting, part-time job focused on a cause that was important to her. Within a few months, Emily was captivated by a handsome, smooth-talking, and self-assured co-worker who was in his thirties. Despite their age difference, they began dating. Jim quickly charmed her with fancy restaurants and impressed her with exciting outings. He professed to be a

Christian and seemed to have all the right answers about life. He was captivating.

For the next two years, Emily and Jim dated as she pursued her bachelor's degree. However, she became progressively concerned regarding his extensive use of alcohol. After deep soul searching, she decided to break off their relationship. After their breakup, Jim continued to pursue Emily for the next six months, almost obsessively. He claimed he had sought professional support and his use of alcohol was now under control. He also promised to attend church with her, fully support her chosen career, and her pursuit of a law degree. All these things were extremely important to her. Emily was naïve and in love. She soon succumbed to his charm and promises as she re-engaged in their relationship.

Jim quickly asked for Emily's hand in marriage, then pushed for a wedding four months later, during her final semester of college. In retrospect, she shared, "It was like a speeding freight train to the altar, and I now know why." Within a few days after their marriage, Jim flew into a fit of rage and anger. Emily was shocked, stunned, and afraid. She had never experienced this type of scary and uncontrolled behavior. In her mind, she tried to excuse his actions as a one-time event due to stress from their marriage and settling into a new lifestyle. Unfortunately, Emily soon learned it was her new reality and way of life.

The next several weeks were drastically different compared to her hopes and dreams for their marriage. Emily did her best to focus on finals, graduation, and securing a job instead of the unexpected drama unfolding at home. She was confused and bewildered as Jim transformed into a different person. His charming disposition disappeared as controlling actions, jealous behaviors, and narcissistic traits dominated his personality; characteristics he somehow managed to conceal from Emily for nearly three years. She began to question herself and her judgment. How did she miss so many issues before their marriage? Unfortunately, his conscious approach toward their relationship soon became crystal clear. One evening, Emily asked to go to dinner or a movie, similar to when they were dating. She was stunned when Jim replied, "No, I don't have to do that anymore. We're married." He proceeded to get drunk and fly into another fit of rage.

After her graduation, Emily landed an exciting job where she could make a difference. Unfortunately, Jim was extremely jealous of her position and her co-workers. After only one year, he pressured her to quit. He also forbade her to attend law school, going against his promise to support her pursuit to become an attorney. Emily was crushed and confused. She was afraid and embarrassed to share her situation with family and friends. After all, she had been married less than eighteen months. What would people think? Emily knew she was in trouble, but kept her fears to herself. She asked God for comfort and safety as she moved forward.

Jim continued his attempts to control Emily by slowly isolating her from family and friends. He became fixated on embarrassing her whenever possible. Privately, he spoke to her in condescending tones and insulted her on every aspect of her life. From cooking to cleaning to general conversations, he made fun of her at every turn. If she tried to stand up for herself or expressed her thoughts, it would release Jim's fury that was hard to describe. It became easier not to push back or try to defend herself. Then, he began to mock her faith and love of God. He routinely sabotaged her attempts to attend church on Sundays. Emily became disheartened and broken. It took all the energy she could muster to make it through each day.

Emily lived her life on eggshells. She never knew what comment or action would trigger his anger and rage. His intentional, mental abuse made her tremble and fear for her life as he mixed his fury with alcohol. She knew this was not how God envisioned marriage or how He wanted women to be treated.

*"Husbands, love your wives, just as Christ loved the church
and gave himself up for her." Ephesians 5:25 (NIV)*

After two years of marriage, Emily was emotionally and physically exhausted. She finally gathered enough courage to get on a plane and fly to her parents' home as she considered a trial separation. This was a huge step for Emily since she did not believe in divorce. Her parents were shocked when they picked her up from the airport. She was covered in hives from the stress and was a shell of her former self. Her mother immediately knew something was drastically wrong. For the next few weeks, Emily shared small insights into her marriage, never completely revealing the severity of her situation. She was too embarrassed. Jim, on the other hand, called several times a day as he charmed her with false promises and apologies. He begged her to return and assured her things would be different as they moved forward with their marriage. Emily once again fell for his charm, hoping and believing he had changed. While her mother begged her not to return, she boarded a plane and flew back to Jim.

For the first few days, things appeared to be better, and she was hopeful. Unfortunately, Jim once again created a false sense of security for Emily, something he had mastered when they were dating. Within a month, she learned she was pregnant with their first child. By that time, the old Jim had fully re-emerged including his drinking, rages, and threats.

In his quest to have total control over her life, he completely ignored the promises he made only a few weeks earlier, and he continued on a path to finish destroying her self-confidence. Emily felt trapped and dreaded each new day. Since she was now expecting a baby, she had no idea how to escape this nightmare. She sought refuge in God through prayer, something Jim could not strip away from her. Eight months later, she gave birth to a beautiful little boy.

> ### *Philippians 4:6-7 (NIV)*
>
> Do not be anxious about anything, but in every situation, by prayer and petition, with thanksgiving, present your requests to God. And the peace of God, which transcends all understanding, will guard your hearts and your minds in Christ Jesus.

For the next ten years, Emily suffered as she endured a painful existence of domestic abuse that came and went. Whenever she relaxed and thought her life might normalize, Jim would suddenly embark on another meltdown. There was no rhyme or reason to his ever-changing behavior.

When a rage episode was finally over, a period of calm often followed. Jim was an expert at making Emily believe things would get better. Unfortunately, as soon as she let her guard down and settled back into a daily routine, his verbal and emotional attacks would commence once again. The emotional roller coaster filled her with anxiety and left her mentally exhausted.

During this same period, Emily was blessed with two additional children. She loved being a stay-at-home mom and believed it was the most important job in the world. In many ways, she raised her children as a single mother due to the numerous challenges with Jim. She focused on building her children's self-esteem and strived to help them feel secure, despite her own self-confidence challenges and insecurities. In her role as a stay-at-home-mom, Emily became very isolated due to Jim's extreme jealousy. He made it nearly impossible for her to socialize.

Emily was able to get out of the house one night a month to volunteer for a cause that was important to her. Sadly, after each monthly meeting, she arrived home to face Jim's explosive temper. He would always accuse her of being somewhere other than the volunteer meeting. It was evident he wanted total control over Emily 24/7 due to his insecurities. While her volunteer work gave her a renewed sense of purpose and fulfillment, she questioned whether it was worth the explosive situation when she returned home. Jim repeatedly attempted to force Emily to stop volunteering, but she held her ground and decided to live with the consequence each month.

While she contemplated leaving Jim numerous times due to the mental and emotional abuse, she struggled with financial constraints compounded by her belief that divorce was a sin. She also feared a divorce would damage her children. She did not want them to grow up in a broken home. Unfortunately, she was unable to realize her married home was already broken and negatively impacting her family. When Jim was home at night or on the weekends, she did everything in her power to shelter her children from his abuse. Emily made excuses for his behavior, so the children were not afraid. She held tightly to her faith in God as He sustained her.

There were many nights when Emily was afraid to fall asleep as the impact of the drama weighed heavily on her heart. On many mornings, she would wake up curled into a fetal position. She shared, "I strived not to make him angry, but it was impossible to determine what would set him off. He always attacked when I was most vulnerable or let my guard down. I can remember thinking, if only I could be a better wife, more attractive, or could lose weight. Perhaps then, just maybe, his wraths of fury would stop." Emily's life was terrifying and sad. A lifestyle God did not condone, but the result of his gift of "free will." Jim chose to be a monster and Emily was trapped in his path. She continued to pray for a way out of her bondage, as she leaned on God for strength, guidance, and comfort.

Fortunately, as time progressed, it became necessary for Emily to return to work and generate some additional income for the family. In retrospect, she knows God had a hand in this first step to her freedom. As she worked outside the home, she began to rebuild her self-esteem and build new friendships with some amazing Christian women. Soon, Emily began to set her pride aside and share some glimpses of her painful existence at home. These amazing women surrounded her with love, prayed for her, and offered valuable advice. They never judged her. "I can't emphasize the importance of my female friendships during my journey. When I think of the famous Footprints Poem, it was God that carried me when I didn't know how to take another step. Then, with precision, He placed an incredible group of women in my life, exactly when I needed them, to help me forward. I will forever be grateful."

Slowly, over time, Emily became more and more confident as she continued to pray for the courage to leave with her children. During this same time, her middle child was diagnosed with a severe learning disability. She had to remain strong. She finally garnered enough confidence to no longer cry or react when Jim launched into his rages. This change took away some of his power over her. Emily had to reserve her emotional energy to take care of her children. Then one day, after nineteen years of marriage, everything changed.

The kids were dressed, excited, and ready to go on a rare family outing. As they quietly waited in the front room, full of anticipation, she went upstairs to tell Jim they were ready to leave. However, he had other plans. He refused to leave and demanded intimacy with her immediately. God gave her the strength and courage to stand up to Jim. She told him no, the children were waiting. She turned her back on him and walked away. Her response sparked a horrendous, hateful rage. He uncontrollably ran after her in a fury of anger as he screamed vulgar profanities in front of their children. Suddenly, with an odd sense of calmness that could only come from God, she looked into his eyes and then mustered up the nerve to grab her purse and keys. She told the kids to quickly get in the car, as she ran behind them. When they were safely in the car, she pressed the door lock with her trembling hand and immediately drove away while trying to catch her breath.

As they quietly sat in the car, a life-changing event occurred. Her eight-year-old daughter broke the silence and said, "Mommy, if my husband ever talked to me that way, I would get a divorce." Emily was stunned at the profound words she heard coming out of the mouth of her little girl, and it jolted her into reality. She suddenly realized the caustic, unhealthy, abusive relationship was also harming her children. She shared, "By staying in the marriage, I realized I was teaching my boys it is acceptable to abuse your wife. I was teaching my daughter it is okay and normal if your husband abuses you. I immediately knew I had to save all of us from this sick way of life. While I did not believe in divorce, I also realized my Heavenly Father did not want me or my children to suffer any longer from domestic abuse."

For the next year, Jim moved into their basement but refused to leave the house. Emily lacked the financial means to leave with her children. While it was still a stressful situation, it gave her relief from his daily abuse and allowed her and the children to attend church without being mocked. Due to her religious beliefs, she pursued marriage counseling with Jim, but it was a disaster. He lied numerous times during the counseling process. They lost their first counselor when Jim launched into a rage during a counseling session. Next, Emily made arrangements for them to meet with a Christian counselor. After several months, the counselor finally told Emily by staying in the marriage she was endorsing and condoning his abuse and use of alcohol. He also assured her she had Biblical grounds for a divorce.

Emily had done everything possible to save the marriage. A few days before she formally separated from Jim, she felt encircled by love and music during a Sunday morning church service. She could feel God supporting her and knew He would protect her. Emily filed for divorce as she embarked on a new life as a single mother with limited income. Their home was placed on the market as Jim was formally given thirty days to move out of the house. Emily and her children remained in their home for the next year until it finally sold.

TACKLING LIFE AS A SINGLE MOM

While Emily did her best to raise their children and keep their lives calm, Jim did everything in his power to make her life miserable. He created issues to force her to communicate with him. One day, her oldest son came home from high school to discover all his bedroom furniture was gone. The room was bare. Emily's son called her office in a panic. She took a deep breath, said a quick prayer, and then calmly assured her son it was okay. She quickly realized Jim took the furniture, but she chose to take the high road. They went out that evening and purchased a bed, mattress, sheets and pillows so her son could once again feel secure in his bedroom. Emily did not have the financial means to cover the unplanned expenses; she trusted God that things would be okay.

As Emily began searching for a small home, she realized, due to Jim's insistence and controlling behaviors, all their business transactions and assets were solely in his name. She lacked her own credit history. As she struggled to care for her family, Emily added a second job to pay bills. She worked hard to quickly establish a positive credit score in her name so she could purchase a home. Expenses were cut and trimmed wherever possible. Extreme couponing and off-brand markets became a way of life for her and the children.

After several months, Jim and Emily's house finally sold. They needed to be out in sixty days. As Emily intensified her search for a home close to their former neighborhood, she was unable to find anything in her price range. She believed it was important for her children to remain at their same schools with their friends. She continued to pray for God's guidance. Suddenly, a house came on the market that was perfect and in her price range. She knew it was the right place when she went into the backyard and looked through the trees. The home backed-up to her church, a confirmation she was doing the right thing. Due to many prayers and an excellent real estate agent, she managed to financially qualify for the house, and her offer was accepted. Emily was thrilled. She would be safe in her own home where Jim would not have access.

Two months later, Emily and her children moved into their new home. She was anxious to move forward. She made arrangements to rent the house for two days as they waited for the sale on their old home to close. As they settled into their small home, full of excitement, Emily received a crushing phone call. The sale of the former home fell through at the last minute, meaning she had no funds to purchase the new house where she was now living. She fell apart and sobbed. She was paralyzed in place. That evening at 9 PM, she had a short phone conversation with her real estate agent. Her agent bluntly stated, "Honey, you can pray, or you can worry. You are choosing to worry." Then, her agent prayed with her and told her to get some sleep.

The next morning, Emily woke up early singing the song "I Surrender All." She then turned to God in prayer and fully surrendered the house and situation to Him. As she let go, she felt an astonishing, cleansing feeling come over her. When Emily got out of bed, she checked her email and was shocked to find a message from her real estate agent saying, "I showed your old house to a family at 10 PM, I am expecting an offer by 8 AM." The family purchased the house, and it closed in thirty days. Emily was able to rent her new home until she received the funds to make her down payment. She shared, "God heard our prayers and performed an amazing miracle that night."

> "But when you ask, you must believe and not doubt,
> because the one who doubts is like a wave of the sea,
> blown and tossed by the wind." James 1:6 (NIV)

For three additional years, Jim refused to sign the divorce paperwork, even though Emily surrendered all her rights to spousal support and benefits. He openly disclosed his goal to ruin her so she would need him financially. After thousands of dollars in attorney fees, he finally signed the divorce papers. Emily had no money in the bank and only a small amount of child support coming in, but she was free. Then one day, she realized, "The Bible does not say your ex-husband will provide for you, it says God will provide for you. I remembered the powerful Bible verse about sparrows and I was suddenly covered in peace."

Matthew 6:26 (NIV)

Look at the birds of the air;
they do not sow or reap
or store away in barns,
and yet your heavenly Father feeds them.

Are you not much more valuable than they?

Bible verses continued to come alive and offer encouragement as Emily and her children moved forward. Her middle son's learning disabilities and challenges were not improving as medical expenses mounted. Despite it all, she strived to focus on her numerous blessings and the freedom God had provided. Focusing on her blessings gave her comfort, joy, and peace.

Philippians 4:8 (NIV)

Finally, brothers and sisters, whatever is true, whatever is noble, whatever is right, whatever is pure, whatever is lovely, whatever is admirable - if anything is excellent or praiseworthy – think about such things.

God continued to meet Emily's needs. Every time she faced financial shortfalls or needed assistance, including mortgage payments, something remarkable happened. The money appeared, or her need was met. She received three separate promotions at work which increased her pay. When she was $5,000 short for her son's college tuition, his great uncle passed away and left him $5,000. When she needed furniture, her needs were met through gifts or inexpensive purchases via Craig's List. When Jim took away her daughter's car, a friend suddenly offered a car at no cost. Her exact needs were met time after time.

Based on her Christian beliefs, Emily realized there was a remaining issue she needed to address. She needed to forgive Jim, but she was still angry, hurt, and bitter. At first, she prayed and asked God to give her the simple desire to forgive Jim, since forgiving him was not high on her list. Slowly and over time, her hardened heart toward Jim began to soften as she continued to pray. She began to realize forgiveness was necessary for herself and her children, but the process of forgiveness took years.

On many occasions, just when she was close to forgiving Jim, he would once again do something cruel, causing her to restart the process of forgiveness all over again. It was a vicious circle. Fortunately, through the grace of God and many bumpy attempts, Emily finally forgave Jim for his years of abuse. The act of forgiveness helped the healing process and removed her heavy load of anger and resentment. It freed her heart and soul from Jim's bondage. However, for her protection and mental welfare, she consciously made the decision to have minimal interactions with him as she proceeded forward on her new, healthy journey.

Emily decided to seek professional counseling to handle her nightmares, flashbacks, and the random events that filled her body with fear and adrenaline. She was diagnosed with post-traumatic stress disorder as a result of her nineteen years of abuse. Christian music became a major part of her recovery process. "I found great comfort in old hymns and new Christian choruses. They helped me get through many tough days. I was so honored to be allowed to openly praise God in my home without fear or mocking. I would get up early each morning just to listen to powerful songs of praise and offer my prayers of thanksgiving. Sometimes as I sang to God, tears would flow down my face, partially from sadness, but primarily from gratitude. I could feel God carrying me as I healed."

"Take delight in the Lord, and he will give you
the desires of your heart." Psalm 37:4 (NIV)

In closing, Emily shared, "God took care of us when I took a bold leap of faith to escape nineteen years of abuse. As I trusted God and leaned on Him for courage and strength, He was always with us. At every turn and bump in the road, you could see His hand in small ways, big ways, and unexpected ways. I know God hates divorce, but I also know He loves divorced people. I will forever be grateful to our loving God for setting us free from the bondage of abuse. I now have peace and joy in my life. Praise God!"

John 14:27 (NIV)

Peace I leave with you;
my peace I give to you.
I do not give to you as the world gives.
Do not let your hearts be troubled
and do not be afraid.

REFLECTION

1. Close your eyes for a moment and reflect on your life. Be completely honest with yourself and don't run away from your thoughts. Shine a light in every corner of your heart and mind. Sit still as you take slow, deep breaths.

    What comes to your mind regarding your personal life?

    _____

    _____

    _____

    _____

2. Are there things or activities going on in your life that concern or embarrass you? Are there things you try to hide from your family, friends, or God?

    _____

    _____

    _____

    _____

3. Have you asked God if He is happy with the way you are living your life? *Yes / No*

    _____

    _____

    _____

    _____

4. As we saw in Emily's story, God showed up numerous times to help her in various ways. There are no such things as a coincidence.

    Pause and Reflect. Have there been times when God helped you? *Yes / No*

    If you answered yes, describe what happened?

    _____

    _____

_____

_____

_____

Did you thank God for helping you? *Yes / No*

NEXT STEPS

1. Do you want to take steps to change your life to align with God's plans for you? *Yes / No*

   If you answered yes, start your "change journey" right now by praying this prayer:

   Dear God,

   Please help me. I want to fulfill your purpose for my life. I know I need to make some changes. I need to (fill in the appropriate blanks):

   - *Start _____*
   - *Stop _____*
   - *Get out of _____*
   - *Seek professional help to deal with _____*

   Please guide and direct me as I take steps to change. Thank you. Amen.

   Depending on your situation, there are a variety of resources available to help you as you move forward including family, friends, support groups, and local churches. If you want or need to seek professional help, below are some additional resources. Remember, you are not alone.

   - If you feel you are in immediate danger, call the police at 911

   - National Domestic Violence Hotline 1-800-799-7233

   - Alcoholics Anonymous®
     http://www.aa.org

- Gamblers Anonymous®
  http://www.gamblersanonymous.org

- Local Women Shelters

- Your local church or hospital can provide you with a list of counselors if you want or need help to overcome abuse or addictions including alcohol, drugs, gambling, pornography, or other challenges you are facing.

CLOSING PRAYER

God is with us 24/7. He reveals Himself to us in many ways. Make sure you take the time to notice and appreciate the small, big, and unexpected ways He helps you every day.

Dear God,

Thank you for the many blessings in my life. When times are tough, and I am in the middle of a personal storm, please help me to remember that you are with me. Thank you for being with me as I move forward and take steps to ensure my life aligns with your plans for me. Thank you for your unconditional love. Amen.

Pushing Through Life's Obstacles

"For I am the Lord your God who takes hold of your right hand and says to you, Do not fear; I will help you."
Isaiah 41:13 (NIV)

It was a tough semester. Despite his learning disabilities, Tyler thought he had classes under control and refused tutoring or extra support. Then, final grades were posted and reality set in. The glaring F's on his report card brought tears to his eyes as his stomach wrenched into a sick knot. A week later, an official suspension letter arrived in the mail. He was kicked out of college. Tyler was devastated. He finally hit rock bottom, or so he thought. Unfortunately, there was more to come.

Tyler was raised as an only child by two loving parents. They were married ten years before his birth. He was the center of their attention from the moment he was born. As a special gift, they chose to name him after a remarkable young Christian man they had known for years. They wanted Tyler to have a role model and mentor he could look up to as he grew. They had no idea how important this simple gesture would be for his life in the years to come.

For the first part of his life, Tyler was surrounded by a large family that lived within ten minutes from his house. Family was very special to him, and he loved the excitement of being around his cousins, aunts, and uncles. He was actively involved in church activities, and his mom taught his Sunday School class. Since both his parents worked, he stayed with his grandparents during the day, where he was loved and enriched in Christian values. When he turned three, he attended pre-school two days a week. Soon, his teachers noticed some differences in his ability to learn. His parents were concerned, so they had his eyes and hearing checked. Other than color blindness, no other concerns were noted.

As the years moved on, Tyler continued to struggle with his ability to learn and retain information. By first grade, despite his efforts to work hard, there was a gap in his ability to process new information. As his parents began to contemplate next steps, a sudden traumatic event occurred while on vacation.

As he sat down with his family to enjoy dinner at a favorite restaurant, Tyler ordered the kids meal which came with carrot sticks. As he took a big bite of a carrot and swallowed, the carrot became lodged in his airway. Unable to breathe or speak, he immediately stood up as the color from his face drained away. Tyler shared, "All of a sudden I was unable to breathe or talk. As my head began to spin, my mind felt very dark, and I was afraid. I thought I was going to die." His father quickly performed the Heimlich maneuver and dislodged the carrot as he gasped for air. Tyler added, "That night, I asked my parents to help me accept Jesus into my heart. I completely understood my request. I wanted Jesus as my personal savior." From that point forward, he felt better, but he now faced a new obstacle. He was afraid to eat.

The choking event threw Tyler into a severe eating disorder. Over the next six months, he lost 25% of his body weight. Finally, after several doctors, Tyler's pastor came to his house and prayed with him. At that precise point, something changed. Tyler's fears diminished, and he began to eat normally again. Even though he was young, he knew God rescued him through his pastor's prayers for help.

By the third grade, Tyler continued to fall further and further behind in school, despite his parents' help. School was hard, and he longed to be like the other kids. He was embarrassed, but he did not know what to do. As Tyler continued to struggle with his ability to read, he privately prayed to God and asked for help every night. Then, an unexpected turn of events occurred. His mother accepted a new job across the country, just as he was diagnosed with a severe learning disability.

At age nine, Tyler's life drastically changed as he moved across the country with his parents, leaving all his friends, family, and pastor behind. He was incredibly sad. Just before school started, his parents had him retested for a learning disability. It was confirmed. He had a short-term memory auditory processing disability which required special education services. He was way behind in all areas of his studies, testing at the nine-percentile compared to his same-aged peers. To his parent's surprise, they learned Tyler's school was located in the country's top school district for learning disabilities. They knew God had a plan for Tyler.

Since he did not know anyone in his new school, at the urging of the school's principal, his parents made the decision to have him repeat the third grade. When they broke the news to Tyler, he was upset, but after a few weeks and many talks with his parents, he felt relieved to have the opportunity to catch up. At his young age, Tyler continued to pray to God and ask for help as he started his new school and repeated the third grade.

At first, Tyler was embarrassed to be pulled out of class for specialized help with his reading, writing, and math. But soon, he realized other kids had challenges too. As the teachers encouraged him, Tyler worked hard to focus on his assignments and learn. He also began to make new friends and adjust to his new home. Before long, his reading and writing showed marked improvement, but he was still far behind the other children. He continued to push through his obstacles, a skill that would help him in the years to come.

As the years passed, Tyler began to realize he was smart, he just learned differently. By the end of eighth grade, things were finally coming together as he looked forward to his freshman year in high school. Then, Tyler faced a major obstacle he never saw coming; a change that would impact his life forever. After twenty-five years of marriage, his parents came in his room one night and shared they were having some problems. His father wanted to leave the marriage. Tyler was devastated. He immediately called his namesake to discuss the situation. His mentor listened compassionately and prayed with him. He also reached out to his grandmother who encouraged him and told him he was loved. That night, as he had learned through his other obstacles, Tyler prayed and asked for help once again. He knew he could not get through his pain and confusion without God. His father moved out the weekend before his first day in high school. The house seemed empty.

Tyler's freshman year was a whirlwind. After his first few weeks in school, he was failing three classes. His learning disability teacher pulled him out of class and bluntly told him to get his act together. He finally opened up and shared his distractions due to his parents' divorce. It was hard to concentrate. He promised to turn things around as his teacher, Ms. Smith, took a personal interest in him and committed to helping him if he stepped up. Tyler believed she was an answer to his prayer; he thanked God for her.

Just as Tyler turned his grades around with the support of Ms. Smith, he learned he required immediate surgery to correct a hernia. His pastor and parents surrounded him as he pulled through the surgery, only missing a few weeks of school. The missed classes again impacted his grades. As the year progressed, his mother slipped into a deep depression, and he prayed for her and himself. Life was hard and different. He was thankful for caring neighbors, his mentor, and his grandmother that talked with him several times a week.

After the divorce, things seemed to normalize until his mother met a man and they began to date. Tyler was very concerned when he met his mother's boyfriend. He immediately sensed something was off. He felt an unspoken level of anger but said nothing because his mother seemed so happy. Unfortunately, after only four months, his mother married the man during the first semester of his sophomore year, and his new step-father moved into their house. Within weeks, the man changed, and they found themselves dealing with verbal and mental abuse. Tyler kept the challenges to himself and prayed.

Despite the challenges at home, Tyler did his best to focus on school with the help of Ms. Smith. He began to hang out with some great kids at school who had similar values. He started to feel like he fit into a group despite his learning challenges. As things began to normalize, his biological father announced his engagement to a much younger woman. Once again, his world turned upside down, but he knew God was with him. He just considered it "Round 2" as he tried to adjust to yet another significant change in his life.

As time passed, he learned his step-mother was pregnant. Tyler was devastated when he realized he would no longer be his father's only child. He was heartbroken and cried. The pregnancy became a heavy burden on his heart. He tried to lean on God for strength as his grades plummeted. His mother, grandmother, Ms. Smith, and his mentor came to his rescue once again. They did their best to shore him up and get him through his junior year.

There were many times when Tyler could have thrown in the towel, but based on his upbringing alcohol and drugs were never an option. He was not interested in pursuing an escape that could potentially ruin his life. He believed there were other options. He shared, "I knew God would come up with a way to help me become comfortable with my new realities in life."

By his senior year, Tyler had a great group of friends. School finally clicked, and he was proud of his accomplishments. His relationship with his step-father slightly improved as he learned some valuable lessons from him regarding work ethics and life. At his step-father's urging, Tyler applied for and accepted a part-time job which significantly improved his self-confidence. He was thrilled when he received the employee of the month award. Tyler also began to appreciate his new role as a big brother. He realized life might work out after all.

Despite his learning challenges, Tyler decided to pursue a college education. Due to some remarkable grades his senior year, he was accepted into a university that had an excellent program for students with disabilities. Tyler's freshman year in college was outstanding. He made new friends as he maintained a strong grade point average due to his disciplined work ethic.

Unfortunately, during his sophomore year, Tyler began to let his studies slip as he tried to approach school like students who did not have a learning disability. He did not want to be different. By the end of his sophomore year, he failed several classes and was kicked out of the university. Tyler was once again devastated as his world fell apart. He knew he let his parents and himself down. He began to fear he would never exceed at anything. His dreams were shattered.

Tyler moved back home as his mother helped him pick up the pieces of his life. They prayed together many times as he tried to lay out a path forward. He enrolled in the local community college as he placed his sights on reapplying to the same university and completing his bachelor's degree. Tyler's plans seemed to be progressing, and he was passing all his classes until he suffered a devastating knee injury playing basketball. Only two weeks before the fall semester finals, Tyler required a total knee reconstruction. He tried to take his final exams, but due to the pain of forty staples in his leg and the fogginess from medications, he failed several of his classes.

Tyler was a mess. He broke down and sobbed. He believed he had finally hit rock bottom and he did not know what to do. He became depressed. Unfortunately, there was more. On his way to physical therapy, he was involved in a car accident. His car was totaled only two days before Christmas. He felt defeated and no longer knew how to move forward.

On New Year's Eve, Tyler spent the evening flat in bed with his leg in a huge, straight brace. He was unable to place any weight on his restructured leg for another two months. As he reflected on his current situation, anxiety once again set in. Then at 3 AM, in the privacy of his bedroom, it suddenly dawned on him the prior year was now behind him. Tyler needed to stop focusing on his failures and move forward, but how? Then, he realized based on all his prior obstacles, from the carrot incident forward, he could turn his life around with God's help.

As he continued to ponder, Tyler finally grasped that leading his own life versus following God's lead was obviously not working. With that new awareness, he pulled himself out of bed and onto the floor. With one knee on the ground and his other leg straight, Tyler bowed his head and surrendered his entire life to God. He talked to God and shared his thoughts and feelings. Then, he asked his Heavenly Father to get his life back on track. When he finished praying, he slowly pulled himself off the floor and back into bed. He then thought, "Alright! God is with me–I feel better." Then Tyler fell into a deep sleep, free from anxiety.

> "Therefore I tell you, whatever you ask for in prayer,
> believe that you have received it, and it will be yours."
> Mark 11:24 (NIV)

From that point forward, Tyler's life changed quickly and dramatically. His step-father made arrangements for Tyler to have a car the next week. His leg healed much faster than anticipated. He passed all his spring semester classes with flying colors as his father helped him re-apply to the same university. After many prayers, Tyler wrote a heartfelt letter to the admissions office sharing the lessons he learned over the past year. Then, the letter from the university's admission office arrived; he was accepted for the fall semester. His mother made special arrangements for Ms. Smith to tutor him via the phone and the internet during his junior and senior year. At every turn, he could see God's hand in little miracles. God led Tyler step by step. He was grateful and hopeful.

When Tyler returned to college, he focused on his studies and sought extra help as required. He was thankful for the second chance to prove himself. Two years later, Tyler made the honor roll and graduated with his bachelor's degree. A month before graduation, he accepted the job he hoped and prayed for, as everything fell into place. God was faithful once again as Tyler trusted his Heavenly Father with his entire life.

In closing, Tyler shared, "I believe in the power of prayer. God heard my pleas for help, and He rescued me numerous times throughout my life. He was with me on my darkest and hardest days. I was never alone. I am extremely thankful for the positive people He placed in my life. They truly care about me and my future." Tyler went on to share, "With God, you can push through obstacles and turn your life around, even when you think there is no hope. Stay strong and just believe!"

REFLECTION

1. Pause and Reflect. Find a quiet place to think about your life. Are there times God carried you through tough or challenging times? *Yes / No*

    If you answered yes, list those times below:

    - _____
    - _____
    - _____
    - _____
    - _____
    - _____
    - _____

2. Things turned around for Tyler when he completely surrendered his challenges to God. Are there times in your life when you completely surrendered your pain and storms to God? If yes, what happened?

    _____
    _____
    _____
    _____
    _____
    _____
    _____

NEXT STEPS

1. Prayer is a powerful gift from God. Sometimes we make prayer complicated. We assume we need to use "special and fancy words" to pray to God, so we wait. Or, we want that special quiet spot where we can pray, so we wait. Or, we don't think we are worthy to pray to God, so we wait. Are you waiting?

The bottom line, you do not need glitzy words to talk with our Heavenly Father! You don't need the perfect place to pray. God loves you just the way you are. He already knows your heart, no matter what you have done. Just simply bow your head, close your eyes and talk to Him using your own words. He is waiting to listen to you. Don't wait. Pray!

2. Tyler recognized and valued the power of prayer. Through prayer we can:

    • Ask God for guidance, direction, and help

    • Request healing for ourselves or others

    • Seek His will and purpose for our lives

    • Ask for strength to get through a heartbreak

    • Request wisdom and courage to move forward despite our obstacles

    • Praise and thank God for our blessings

    • What else comes to your mind regarding prayer?

    _____

    _____

    _____

    _____

    _____

    _____

    _____

3. Do you want to surrender something to God? *Yes / No*

    If you answered yes, what issues, habits, situations, challenges, or heartaches do you want to surrender?

_____

_____

_____

_____

_____

_____

_____

_____

_____

CLOSING PRAYER

You can spend time with God by praying right now. Don't put if off! He is patiently waiting to hear your voice.

Dear God,

I need your help. I want to surrender _____ to you. Trying to handle _____ on my own is not working. From this point forward, I am trusting you. Please guide and direct me on my next steps as I follow you. Thank you. Amen.

Embracing Down Syndrome

"Trust in the Lord with all your heart and lean not on your own understanding; in all your ways submit to him, and he will make your paths straight." Proverbs 3:5-6 (NIV)

After several months of praying and waiting, she was finally pregnant. Heather and Scott were thrilled at the thought of welcoming their third child into this world. As the weeks went on, hopes and dreams started to emerge for their unborn baby that they already loved.

Due to a miscarriage in her eleventh week on Christmas Eve three years earlier, they were cautiously optimistic that this pregnancy would proceed smoothly with no complications. At her eleven-week doctor appointment, they conducted routine blood tests and performed a baseline ultrasound. Soon after the ultrasound was complete, the doctor quietly came into the room to address some concerns. Fear filled their minds as the doctor began to share the ultrasound results.

"A physical abnormality has been identified. A genetic disorder is expected in your baby." The doctor's words seemed frozen in time. While they lacked conclusive details, there was strong evidence pointing toward Down Syndrome. The baby also had a very large cystic hygroma that was attached from its neck to the middle of its back. Due to the sizable cyst, there was a high probability that it would overcome the baby, resulting in Heather miscarrying in the upcoming weeks. The news was overwhelming and shocking.

Their heads were spinning as they met with the genetic counselor immediately after the doctor broke the frightening news. While the counselor was empathic, she was also very direct about the serious issues facing the baby. Potential options were touched upon and discussed regarding the pregnancy and next steps. It was implied they could immediately terminate the pregnancy or they could move forward with the strong potential that the baby would self-terminate. At sixteen weeks, if the pregnancy was still viable, they could conduct an amniocentesis as well as a genetic sonogram to gather conclusive genetic results regarding their baby. The risk associated with the amniocentesis testing was also described.

Due to the shocking events of the day, Heather and Scott were exhausted and were in no frame of mind to make any decisions. They chose to go home, sleep on the devastating news, and pray. This situation was much bigger than they were. They needed and wanted to seek God's guidance, direction, and strength for their next steps. They were afraid of what the future held.

The next five weeks were emotional, raw, and gut wrenching. Every day, Heather would awake and wonder if this would be the day she would miscarry. Then, fear would flood her heart as she speculated what the future held if their baby survived, this baby that they already loved. The unknown was very scary. Were they strong enough to handle what faced them? Day after day, they did their best to pray and trust God as they leaned on Him for strength and shelter from their fears.

They both knew the genetic issues were not from God but were the result of the fact that we live in a fallen world. They also knew from their Christian belief that our all-powerful God could transform heartbreaking events into blessings. They gained daily comfort from God's promises in the Bible and learned to rely on the prayers of their family and friends.

As they approached the sixteenth week, the time came to make decisions about the pregnancy or face the next phase of testing.

Scott shared, "Heather and I knew we could push the easy button by terminating the pregnancy to make all our concerns and fears immediately disappear. We had two choices, take the easy road or trust God. Together, we chose to ruthlessly trust God. We knew He had a plan and held our future in the palm of His hand."

A sense of peace surrounded them as they attended their sixteen-week doctor appointment. They shared their decision not to terminate the pregnancy and forego the amniocentesis testing due to the potential miscarriage risk. They chose to embrace and love their baby, no matter what challenges or issues the future held. The doctor was surprised at the calmness they displayed, but Heather and Scott knew God was in control.

They proceeded with the genetic sonogram and discovered some surprising results. They were having a boy, but some of the key physical markers for Down Syndrome were no longer obvious. Many times, children with Down Syndrome have heart defects, but their baby's heart was perfect. The doctors were also astonished the baby's large cystic hygroma had disappeared. They finally had some positive news, despite her blood tests that indicated there was a high probability of a genetic disorder.

"Be joyful in hope, patient in affliction, faithful in prayer."
Romans 12:12 (NIV)

As Heather's emotional pregnancy continued, she did her best to battle through her daily fears while leaning on God for His peace and strength. She would quietly sing the song "It Is Well with My Soul" as she fought through her tears and sadness with God's help. It was not an easy journey. As the months went on, the doctors were unclear as to whether their son had Down Syndrome. Uncertainty and emotional rollercoasters became the norm. By her seventh month of pregnancy, she came to a point where God's peace superseded her fear. Both she and Scott learned to continually go back to the well of God's strength and unconditional love. They were thankful.

Then, the time came. Heather gave birth to a beautiful, cute baby boy named Maverick. It no longer mattered if he had Down Syndrome because he was perfect in their eyes and they loved him unconditionally. Maverick had no obvious physical markers indicating a chromosome abnormality, his heart was perfect, and he was completely healthy. The doctors were unsure if he had a genetic disorder. They left the hospital not knowing.

Two weeks later, Maverick's blood tests finally came back and confirmed that indeed he had Down Syndrome. However, Heather and Scott were no longer afraid. Their decision to trust God had already paid off. As Scott shared, "This little guy is one of the biggest blessings we have in our life. We know God is with us as we move forward."

Maverick is now a three-year-old bundle of love, high energy, and joy. Yes, he faces learning and physical challenges, but he is happy every day. He enjoys music and dancing. Maverick is a kind, well-mannered, and sensitive little boy that loves everyone around him. In short, he is a blessing from God.

Scott and Heather shared, "If we had terminated the pregnancy, we would have missed out! We are thankful and blessed that God chose us to be Maverick's parents. He enriches our family every day and teaches us humbling, life lessons on an on-going basis. We have learned to be present and appreciate the little things in life. We trust God. We know He will carry us through this journey."

Everyone is special in God's eyes. No matter what a person looks like or what disabilities they may have, everyone deserves to be loved. Maverick may not grow up to be a rocket scientist, but he will grow up knowing he is deeply loved by God and his family.

In closing, fear and doubt will blind you from seeing the potential of God's plans for your life. When the storms hit, you need to quickly surrender your fears to God and let Him carry you through. God is good and faithful. Trust Him! Amen!

"May the God of hope fill you with all joy and peace as you trust him, so that you may overflow with hope by the power of the Holy Spirit." Romans 15:13 (NIV)

Maverick and His Family

Enjoying Christmas Together

A SPECIAL THOUGHT

LynnMarie Rink collaborated with Tom Douglas to write "He Never Will Be." The song and video celebrate the lives of some wonderful, special needs children and their families. Maverick and his family were honored to be part of this heart-touching production. Listen carefully to the powerful words as you reflect on the story above.

https://lynnmarie.bandcamp.com/track/he-will-never-be

REFLECTION

1. Heather and Scott trusted God completely.

   Pause and reflect. What would your life look like if you trusted God with ALL your heart, soul, and mind?

   _____
   _____
   _____
   _____
   _____
   _____
   _____

2. What is stopping you from completely trusting God with your life?

   _____
   _____
   _____
   _____
   _____
   _____

NEXT STEPS

1. Think about your life as you look forward. What are you afraid of?

_____

_____

_____

_____

_____

_____

2. Do you want to turn your fears over to God and fully trust Him?
   Yes / No

   Do you want to fully trust God with your life going forward?
   Yes / No

_____

_____

_____

_____

_____

   If you answered yes, then pray the simple prayer below.

CLOSING PRAYER

Dear God,

Thank you for loving me unconditionally. Help me to open my heart and release my fears to you. I know they are blinding me from seeing and fulfilling your purpose for my life. Thank you for replacing my fears with your strength, peace, love, and hope. Please help me to fully trust you with all aspects of my life as I move forward. I love you. Amen.

Moving Forward After a Bad Decision

"Your Father knows what you need before you ask him."
Matthew 6:8 (NIV)

The police officer grabbed her arm! "We've been watching you. Come with us." A crowd began to assemble as Violet, now twenty-one, was handcuffed in the center of the shopping mall. She was quickly escorted down a long, private, cement corridor and was stunned as the police officer began to read her Miranda rights. As the inquisition process commenced in the mall's satellite police station, it became apparent she was in serious trouble. Violet had been caught. She was videotaped while shoplifting three dresses from two separate stores. "Did you shoplift?" the police officer asked sternly and directly. She looked the police officer in the eye and quietly replied, "Yes," then dropped her head. As they opened Violet's large handbag to obtain her identification, they slowly pulled out the expensive dresses, one at a time. The dresses that she hoped would make her feel better about herself.

As Violet's nightmare continued to unfold, the police officer escorted her down another cold, isolated hallway. As she was placed in the backseat of the police car wearing handcuffs, she started to sob hysterically on her way to the county jail. Then thoughts began to rush through her mind. "What have I done? What will my family think of me? What about college? What about my career aspirations?" After being officially booked and charged with felonies, she was led to a small, dirty jail cell where she was required to change into a green jumpsuit. Fighting away tears, she obeyed the orders to change and quietly handed her clothes to the police officer. After calling her mother to request bail, she sat all alone in the jail cell and waited.

Violet's challenges began to unfold ten years earlier. As an only child, she was blessed with the affection of two devoted parents. Her mother stopped working to dedicate more time to Violet's education and to support her after she was diagnosed with a learning disability. She was a happy child and enjoyed going to school, playing soccer, and participating in family activities with her parents, grandparents and extended family. From her perspective, life was great! It's Mom, Dad, and me – "The Three Musketeers" surrounded by a loving family. Unfortunately, her life was about to change drastically.

Violet noticed her parents were arguing and yelling on a regular basis but assumed this was a normal part of marriage. Then one cold, snowy afternoon, without notice, her parents sat her down and bluntly said, "We are getting a divorce." That night, her father moved out as her mother sobbed uncontrollably. From that day forward, her life was never the same. Her world was shattered at age eleven. "The Three Musketeers" were gone and she was afraid. After her father left, Violet's unemployed mother slipped into a state of depression.

The next year was a blur as Violet's father moved in with his mistress and her children. The relationship with her father deteriorated as he diverted his attention toward his new family. She was further traumatized when she accidentally saw her dad in bed with his mistress and was required to testify at the divorce proceedings to explain what she observed. Violet told the truth to the judge. Unfortunately, her paternal grandparents disowned their only grandchild for telling the truth and being disloyal to their son. Her father was also angry and cut off nearly all communications with her. Violet was confused and upset.

During this same time, Violet's unemployed mother slipped into a deeper depression and stopped providing basic care and support including cooking, shopping, and cleaning. They were required to move out of their home and transition into affordable housing located in a noisy, rough neighborhood several miles away. Violet was forced to leave her remaining support system—her school, friends, and safe neighborhood. She felt out of place and isolated.

Unfortunately, there were more challenges to come. Her mother was diagnosed with cancer. Violet's insecurities, anxiety, and fears of abandonment intensified. Her father and grandparents had abandoned her, and now her mother had cancer. She was afraid and felt alone. For the next several months, her mother went through tests and cancer treatments until she finally received a "clean bill of health." Violet was grateful.

Hopeful that life would find its way to some new normal, Violet soon realized her depressed mother had become obsessed with on-line dating. Her mother just wanted to be loved. She would spend hours searching for men to date; there were piles of dating profiles thrown throughout the house. By age fourteen, Violet fended for herself on the weekends as her mother explored new relationships and worked a part-time job. At first, it was uncomfortable to be alone, but her dog provided protection and helped Violet overcome some of her fears. She remembers eating a lot of cereal, oatmeal, and chips during this period.

From age sixteen until her high school graduation, Violet was alone much of the time. She felt abandoned by both her parents and resented them for it. She found some comfort in spending time with her mother's family, her high school soccer team, and new Christian friends. She also joined an organization called Young Life where she sang, participated in events, and learned Bible verses. A level of faith was always present, but she felt angry, alone, and abandoned. Violet did not recognize God. She felt insecure and unworthy of love. It was difficult for her to trust people.

It was during Violet's senior year of high school that a loving aunt began to take a special interest in her. Her aunt assisted with college applications, financial aid, and began to invite her more frequently to family outings and activities. Violet observed how her aunt and uncle adored their children. She wondered what was wrong with her? Why did her parents treat her so differently? She felt unworthy of love. How could anyone possibly like her, let alone love her?

Despite the challenges, Violet was accepted into a prominent university and was doing very well with her academics during her freshman and sophomore years. Socially, however, she felt unworthy to have friends. She believed she was not good enough and had a difficult time "fitting in" even though she joined a sorority and seemed to have friends. Violet would tell people what she thought they wanted to hear, rather than what she felt or the truth. She wanted desperately to belong. It was during this time that Violet began to shoplift. She knew from her upbringing and Catholic Catechism classes that stealing was wrong. She felt guilty, which only complicated her self-esteem challenges.

And then her life seemingly started to fall into place. Violet landed an exciting six-month internship her junior year with a Fortune 200 company. Life was looking up until that fateful afternoon when she was arrested for shoplifting. Her internship and her college degree were now in jeopardy as she faced jail time and a damaged reputation.

Now anxious and pessimistic about her future, Violet decided to take ownership of her errors and face her issues with transparency. She openly and honestly told the people she cared about in her life what she had done and that she was sorry. She obtained an attorney (that she paid for) and worked within the criminal justice system to get her felonies reduced to misdemeanors. This allowed her to avoid jail time by completing a focused community service program. Violet realized she needed help, so she obtained a counselor to try to understand why she shoplifted and why she felt unworthy to be loved. She wanted to change.

As the weeks passed, she began to share how she felt with her mother; her mother listened, and their relationship began to blossom. She also garnered the strength to call the Human Resources manager at the Fortune 200 company where she had been offered the internship. She openly explained what she had done and respectfully requested a chance to prove herself. After much deliberation, they granted Violet the internship because of her honesty and the steps she had taken to make amends and seek help. Despite all these actions, she still felt alone and did not see how she would ever overcome her criminal record. She was disconnected from God and did not feel His sense of comfort. She was ashamed.

When Violet reported for her internship, God blessed her with an amazing Christian manager that understood the errors she had made and began to mentor her. Shortly after her first day, he sent her a Bible passage in an email that literally changed her life:

Matthew 6:28–34 (NIV)

And why do you worry about clothes? See how the flowers of the field grow. They do not labor or spin. Yet I tell you that not even Solomon in all his splendor was dressed like one of these. If that is how God clothes the grass of the field, which is here today and tomorrow is thrown into the fire, will he not much more clothe you—you of little faith?

So do not worry, saying, "What shall we eat?" or "What shall we drink?" or "What shall we wear?" For the pagans run after all these things, and your heavenly Father knows that you need them.

But seek first his kingdom and his righteousness, and all these things will be given to you as well. Therefore, do not worry about tomorrow, for tomorrow will worry about itself. Each day has enough trouble of its own.

This simple email from a caring and observant manager was Violet's "ah-ha" moment. It opened her eyes and changed her life forever. She realized God loved her and there was hope.

In retrospect, Violet now understands God met her at her weakest moment and created a path for her to have a second chance. She now knows:

- God loves all of us despite our flaws and errors.

- There will be struggles in life, but God has a path for us, and He will encourage us along the way.

- We need to open our minds and our hearts to God's guidance and direction by reading the Bible and praying daily.

Today, Violet has a counselor that works with her every week to help her overcome her past insecurities and hurts. Her relationship with her mother has been restored and is the best it has been in years. While her father is not part of her life, she knows her Father in Heaven is always there for her 24/7. God is strong, and Violet can trust Him. He will be there when the going gets tough. He will never abandon her, let her down, or disappoint her.

God has a plan for our lives no matter what we have lived through or what bad decisions we have made. We simply need to trust our Heavenly Father and seek his guidance on a daily basis.

REFLECTION

1. Have you ever made a bad decision that impacted you? If yes, what decision(s) did you make?

_____

_____

_____

_____

_____

_____

_____

2. What were the consequences of your poor decision(s)?

_____

_____

_____

_____

_____

_____

_____

NEXT STEPS

1. Do you want to ask God to forgive you for the decision(s) you made? *Yes / No*

If yes, pray the simple prayer below:

CLOSING PRAYER

Dear Heavenly Father,

Thank you for loving me and never abandoning me. Please forgive me for the mistakes and bad decisions I have made. Specifically, I ask you to forgive me for:

- _____
- _____
- _____
- _____
- _____
- _____
- _____
- _____
- _____

I am sorry. Please give me strength and wisdom to not repeat my past mistakes. Thank you for being in my corner. Please help and guide me as I move forward in life. I love you! Amen!

Overcoming Pride
and Rebuilding Self-Esteem

*"So do not fear, for I am with you; do not be dismayed, for
I am your God. I will strengthen you and help you;
I will uphold you with my righteous right hand."*
Isaiah 41:10 (NIV)

Mary was excited. Out of town friends were arriving tonight. As she rushed around the house taking care of last minute details, she paused for a moment to get the mail, something her husband usually liked to handle. As she quickly pulled a handful of mail from the mailbox, she began sorting through the stack of envelopes with her fingertips. Suddenly, she slowed down, then paused and thought, "That's odd." A long, white envelope from a different credit card company was addressed solely to her husband. Mary carefully pulled the envelope from the stack, opened it, and began reading the expenses detailed on the bill. As her eyes began to fill with tears and her stomach tightened into a sick knot, she continued to read the long list of charges. The moment seemed to be frozen in time. Expensive local hotel rooms, jewelry purchases, dinners, and gifts were all clearly recorded on the itemized bill – purchases made by her husband without her knowledge. It suddenly became crystal clear, "Oh no...my husband is having an affair."

By all appearances, Mary had a perfect life – impressive job, devoted husband for over twenty years, great family, beautiful house, etc. However, her world as she knew it was about to unravel. Mary noticed her husband was spending large amounts of time on the internet and would change the screen when she entered the room. His phone calls, late meetings, and business trips had increased, but she assumed he was working hard. Whenever she mentioned his additional time away from home, he seemed to have valid excuses, and she felt guilty for questioning him. Unfortunately, she soon learned her suspicions were correct. Not only was her husband involved with multiple women, but he also took thousands of dollars from their line of credit to pay for prostitutes, pornography, first class plane trips, limousines, gifts, and exclusive events. He even booked a local hotel room to include a rose petal turn-down service complete with champagne and strawberries. To make her nightmare worse, her husband used their church tithe money to help cover his deceitful lifestyle. Mary was shocked, devastated, and embarrassed. How could she have been so blind? Had their entire marriage been one big lie? What was wrong with her? What would other people think?

Mary did her best to take care of her family, both emotionally and financially, while concealing her husband's double life. He soon left her for a much younger woman, and they were divorced. Mary was ashamed, mortified, and fearful of what people would think and say. Despite her feelings of embarrassment, rejection, and not feeling "good enough," she stood firm and focused on her faith in the Lord and moved forward. She knew God loved her as she embraced her cornerstone Bible verse:

> "I can do all things through him (Christ) who
> gives me strength." Philippians 4:13 (NIV)

Unfortunately, while Mary was in a very vulnerable state, a strong man who professed to be a Christian came into her life. He swept her off her feet with kind gestures, nice words, and support. He started to attend church with her. Then, after a short romantic courtship, they were married. Regrettably, within a few days after she said "I do," he drastically changed. From that point forward,

Mary endured years of mental and emotional abuse but kept it to herself because of her personal pride and embarrassment. She did not want to have a second failed marriage. What would people think of her?

Mary was afraid of her husband. Fear, anxiety, and "living on egg shells" became her normal lifestyle. While he never physically hit her, he scarred her with deep emotional wounds. She survived in an environment of control, possessiveness, threats, screaming, humiliation, and constant criticism. He told her she was dumb, stupid, and naïve. He would make fun of her lack of confidence and embarrass her in front of people. She carefully censored her words before she spoke to avoid conflict and began wondering what was wrong with her. Mary did what she could to isolate her family from the abuse and made excuses for his behavior. It became easier to not attend church due to the conflict it triggered. She became isolated. No matter how hard she tried, she was never good enough. She learned to block the abusive events from her mind so she could get up the next day and function.

Mary never knew what would send him into a rage. He was unpredictable. Things as simple as not returning the car seat to the right position, moving a piece of paper, or throwing out spoiled food from the refrigerator without his permission could unleash his wrath of anger. While traveling in the car, she was not allowed to talk or ask for a bathroom stop. One time she was in such agony from needing a bathroom, she was unable to walk due to the pain. When she was allowed to get out of the car on a road trip, she was timed. If she came back one minute late, the next hour would be hell. It was an awful existence. Her only elements of self-esteem were found at work, where she continued to "put on a happy face" and excel. However, her husband was now aggressively pushing Mary to quit her job. She felt as if her life was disappearing right before her eyes. She was becoming invisible and non-existent.

Then in the midst of her turmoil, Mary received a surprise layoff notice from work due to a significant overhead reduction. She was devastated. Her job was the only identity she had left. Her self-worth was destroyed. She was not good enough for her first husband, her second husband treated her like a piece of garbage, and now her job had been stripped away from her. She was depressed and could no longer feel God's presence in her life. She was unable to find the energy to pray for herself. Mary knew she needed help, but did not know what to do. It was at this point she began to open up to a few family members and close friends. They started to pray for Mary and provide guidance.

At the suggestion of her mother, Mary went to see her Pastor. After a few minutes of explaining the environment in which she had been living, her Pastor interrupted her. He looked her straight in the eyes, then firmly stated God never intended for one of His children to be subjected to such mental abuse. Mary paused as his comments shocked her. At that moment, her heart was jolted and after seven years of abuse, she "woke up" and finally faced the truth. Soon after this, Mary was physically attacked by a mentally ill person resulting in a severe concussion. Her husband never came to her bedside.

For the next year, Mary moved forward with her eyes wide open and began to meet with a marriage counselor. After many requests, her husband finally agreed to attend a session. Mary did her best to stand up for her rights despite her fears. Her husband became increasingly angry with her, but she did not budge. She held her ground, and he started to have panic attacks. She could feel the power of prayer surrounding her. She knew God was with her. Mary was unwilling to file for divorce due to her Christian beliefs, but then a gift from God came. One evening, she shared her situation with two amazing women from her church. Together they locked arms and boldly prayed that God would make her husband extremely uncomfortable and force him to change or leave the marriage. Three weeks later, her husband filed for divorce because she would no longer be submissive to his abusive control. Due to a prenuptial agreement, the divorce was final two weeks later. She praised God for his gift of freedom but mourned the realization that she had a second failed marriage.

Three months after the divorce, Mary discovered her now ex-husband was involved with their marriage counselor. While devastating, it lit a fire in her like never before, and she became angry. Before the divorce, she had shared her most intimate thoughts with this counselor, and the counselor took advantage of her vulnerable situation. However, there was good news. She trusted God, and He had her in the palm of His hand. Mary was alive, and her heart was beating strong. She remembered God could and would transform her broken heart and shattered self-esteem. He would not abandon her as He knit her back together. He had a purpose for her life, and she wanted to fulfill it. Mary was no longer someone's doormat, and she was on a mission! Satan had sought to emotionally wound and destroy Mary's self-esteem, confidence, and self-worth, but God prevailed! She had a new vision through God's eyes.

Mary began to read the Bible daily and listen to God's voice. She finally realized she had measured herself by the world's definition of success versus God's definition of success. So, she decided to set her pride and embarrassment aside and shine a light on her painful experiences. She now understood Satan wanted her to remain in the darkness of pride where he had total control. Never again! She filed a formal grievance on the counselor for her unethical behavior and won. She re-engaged with family and friends that she had been forced to abandon during her abusive marriage. She accepted a new, dream job which focused on helping people while providing her with a renewed sense of hope and energy. She once again fully engaged with her church and actively contributed her time and talents.

Mary was alive again, but she was different. As a result of the painful events in her life, she now had a new awareness and empathy for people who were hurting. She realized God never left her side. He rescued her from the "free will" choices and decisions the people around her had made. He leveraged her painful experiences to refine her for new work as an advocate and voice for the discouraged.

Mary's life came into full focus one fall afternoon as she quietly overlooked the Gettysburg Battleground at Seminary Ridge. As the wind tousled her hair, she observed how the storm clouds cast large shadows on the battlefield in front of her. Then, an interesting phenomenon started to occur. As the wind blew the clouds across the sky, light broke through. The dark shadows were replaced with waves of light beams that briskly danced across the fields over and over again. The breathtaking rays of light triumphed over the shadows every time. As this occurred, she suddenly realized the battlefield represented her life here on earth. The shadows represented the storms, hardships, and challenges in her life. Every time the shadows had been replaced by the light and love of God. God was faithful and restored her brokenness. As this realization embraced her thoughts, she noticed a large hawk out of the corner of her eye as it took flight over the battlefield. As it soared into the sky toward the light, Mary remembered a great passage in the Bible:

> ### Isaiah 40:28-31 (NIV)
>
> Do you not know? Have you not heard? The Lord is the everlasting God, the Creator of the ends of the earth. He will not grow tired or weary, and his understanding no one can fathom. He gives strength to the weary and increases the power of the weak. Even youths grow tired and weary, and young men stumble and fall; but those who hope in the Lord will renew their strength. They will soar on wings like eagles; they will run and not grow weary,they will walk and not be faint.

Before Mary left the battlefield, she quietly reflected on the thousands of soldiers who lost their lives at Gettysburg and the blood stains that must have covered the grass during those horrific days. She then remembered how Jesus shed his blood on the cross for her sins so that she could have everlasting life. She was grateful. Her heart was overflowing with love and adoration for the Lord.

"For God so loved the world, that he gave his only begotten Son, that whoever believeth in him should not perish, but have everlasting life." John 3:16 (KJV)

In closing, Mary shared, "Don't ever let pride or self-esteem challenges separate you from God's plan for your life. He will faithfully carry you through your storms if you let Him; it is your choice. Remember—God is on your side!"

REFLECTION

1. God does not want anyone to be a victim of mental, emotional, or physical abuse. If you are currently living in an abusive relationship or if you are experiencing the effects of flashbacks due to prior abuse, reach out and get help. Tell a family member, friend, pastor, boss, or counselor.

   If you feel you are in immediate danger, call 911. The 24/7 National Domestic Violence Hotline is 1-800-799-7233. Remember God loves you. You are not alone!

2. Is your pride preventing you from seeking help or sharing your challenges with others? *Yes / No*

   If you answered yes, you have already taken the critical first step of self-awareness. Take a moment and reflect on the ways your self-pride is negatively impacting your life.

   _____

   _____

   _____

   _____

NEXT STEPS

1. Go back to the answers you provided in Step 2 above. The Bible states:

   "Each one should test their own actions. Then they can take pride in themselves alone, without comparing themselves to someone else." Galatians 6:4 (NIV)

   When pride takes over our lives in the form of embarrassment, conceit, or arrogance, it can become rich territory for Satan. It can prevent you from seeking the help or assistance you need. Do you need to make some adjustments in your self-pride?

   _____

   _____

_____

_____

2. How do you define self-esteem?

_____

_____

_____

_____

3. How can you strengthen your self-esteem to fulfill God's purpose for your life? Do you need additional training, support, or help? Take a moment and reflect.

_____

_____

_____

_____

4. What steps are you willing to take this week to ensure your pride and self-esteem are healthy in the eyes of the Lord?

_____

_____

_____

_____

CLOSING PRAYER

Dear God,

Thank you for loving me. Help me to remember to look up to you for direction and guidance versus the world for affirmation. I love you. Amen.

Trusting God for Strength

"For he himself is our peace..." Ephesians 2:14 (NIV)

Tears quietly rolled down Dede's cheeks. Bobby was the love of her life, and now he was gone. As she hugged the family members who had gathered around his hospital bed, she did her best to hold herself together. After all, she promised Bobby five years earlier she would remain strong. As she left his room for the last time, she realized life was going to be drastically different without her husband and best friend.

Dede and Bobby first met in high school when they sat beside each other during a Civil War history class their senior year. Bobby was very popular due to his athletic accomplishments and had a contagious, outgoing personality. Dede was a conscientious and focused student who was quite mature for her age. The two of them quickly established a friendship. It became an on-going joke that Bobby could never remember to bring a pen or pencil to class and Dede routinely came to his rescue. The fun bantering back and forth soon lit a spark between the two of them. They started dating a few months later, but went their separate ways after graduation, attending colleges in different states. Despite the distance between them, they enjoyed a special bond and remained in contact over the next few years. By their junior year, they decided to no longer date other people and focused on their long-distance relationship.

Upon college graduation, Dede and Bobby went to Europe for two months to see the world. On their return, Bobby moved to North Carolina to support the Volunteers in Service to America (VISTA) where he established education programs for inmates at the Rowan County minimum-security prison. Dede, on the other hand, landed a job with a Fortune 500 company and lived with her parents in Virginia. One year later, Bobby returned home to accept a teaching position at a local Catholic school. They were finally together again. Their love continued to grow, and life was great until they both had the shock of their lives.

In the spring of 1979, Bobby found a lump under his arm. He did not want to scare Dede unnecessarily, so he did not mention it. After all, he was twenty-four and in great shape. Bobby's father, however, was a doctor and he immediately took control of the situation. He was very concerned about the lump since cancer ran in their family. Unfortunately, medical tests soon revealed that Bobby had Stage 2 Hodgkin's Lymphoma.

Dede was devastated when Bobby broke the news. They were in love and assumed their entire lives were in front of them, but in an instant, everything changed. The thought of cancer was terrifying. However, there was good news. They believed in God and the power of prayer. Together with family and friends, they prayed for Bobby to be healed. Dede shared, "I don't know how people get through devastating and scary events in their lives without faith. I chose to let go of my fears, even when I didn't know how. I turned my fears over to God and simply said, God, I'm with you on this one."

God surrounded them with a sense of peace as they moved forward on their faith-filled journey together. Bobby started the prescribed treatment to kill the cancer growing in his young body. First, his spleen was removed, and then radiation treatments commenced leaving his skin burned. He was in pain but held on to hope through the power of prayer. By fall, radiation treatments were declared successful, and Bobby's cancer was in remission.

They were extremely grateful and praised God. With the "all clear" from the doctors, Bobby asked Dede to marry him in December 1979, nearly seven years after their first date. Of course, she said yes, and wedding plans began.

In the spring of 1980, Bobby's periodic cancer check-up did not go as planned. Based on some borderline test results and his family's history of cancer, the doctors recommended chemotherapy. They did not know the long-term effects of the medication, but there was a strong possibility Bobby and Dede would never have children. Together, they trusted God's plan for their lives and moved forward. Through their faith in Him, they were growing spiritually, both individually and as a couple, despite the challenges facing them.

For the next eight months, Bobby endured chemotherapy treatments on Fridays but devotedly returned to teach English at the Catholic high school every Monday morning. He never gave up. People continued to pray for Bobby's full recovery as their wedding plans moved forward. Finally, the chemo treatments were complete, and the cancer was in full remission. Their prayers were answered again, and they thanked God. As part of their wedding preparation, they wrote letters to each other talking of their hopes and dreams for their marriage and future together. They were married in June 1981.

As time moved forward, they embraced every day as a gift from God and thanked Him for their time together. They dedicated their lives to God and each other. Despite their faith, there was always a feeling in the back of their minds that they were living on borrowed time; perhaps it was Satan trying to keep them off-balanced in an attempt to steal their peace and joy. Regardless, they knew firsthand how precious life was; there were no guarantees.

Bobby started to achieve "cancer free" milestones. First one year, then three, five, ten, twenty, and twenty-five years. God had blessed them and answered their prayers. The further they moved down the road from the original cancer diagnosis, the more their lives seemed to normalize without fear. While they were never blessed with children, they relished their time with family and friends. They cherished life together and lived it to the fullest.

In 2005, an unexpected bump in the road surfaced. Bobby started to experience heart problems as a direct result of the life-saving radiation he received years earlier. Unfortunately, the radiation had damaged his arteries, and they were starting to collapse. After three separate stent surgeries, the doctors determined open heart surgery was required. Bobby recuperated and returned to work shortly after open heart surgery, and their lives continued to move forward. They were again grateful.

Then, in July 2008, after twenty-nine years of "cancer free" living, an unexpected event hit them like a ton of bricks. Dede was on a two-week business trip for training when Bobby called saying he thought he had food poisoning. After a few days had passed, he was still sick, so he made a routine doctor's appointment. He told Dede everything was fine, but reality set in when her training class came to a close, and he picked her up at the airport on Friday evening.

Bobby shared the devastating news. He was diagnosed with Stage 4 Non-Hodgkin's lymphoma. Dede fell apart the moment she heard his words. She sobbed throughout the weekend as she fought to overcome her fears and sadness. As the weekend came to a close, Dede realized she did not have enough energy, wisdom, or strength to move forward on her own. She prayed and asked God to "give her enough strength so she could be what Bobby needed." After she had prayed, she pulled herself together, apologized to Bobby for falling apart, and committed to remain strong as they fought his cancer together once again. She reaffirmed her decision to completely and wholeheartedly turn her life over to God and trust Him 100% for her strength, wisdom, energy, and peace day after day.

As testing progressed, the positron emission tomography (PET) scan revealed Bobby's fifty-two-year-old body was filled with cancer. It was everywhere. As they scheduled treatment plans including aggressive chemotherapy, Bobby found himself in unchartered territory. He had always been a very spiritual and private person. He embraced and believed in the power of prayer. However, when he was diagnosed with cancer for the second time, he could no longer find the words to talk with God. He desperately wanted to pray and offer prayers of praise, hope, and requests for his healing, but it was as if his well went dry. He feared he no longer knew how to pray and he was disheartened.

It was at this time, his family and friends stepped in and sustained Bobby through prayer. He also sought guidance and support from his priest who prayed with him, gave him ideas on ways to talk with God, and recommended a little book of prayers for hope and comfort. It was through his prayer journey that both Bobby and Dede embraced the Prayer of St. Francis de Sales. They found it to be extremely consoling and comforting when they read it together. It gave them renewed strength and hope in God's promises and His unconditional love for them.

Prayer of St. Francis de Sales

Do not look forward in fear to the changes of life;
Rather look to them with full hope that as they arise,
God, whose very own you are,
will lead you safely through all things;
And when you cannot stand it,
God will carry you in His arms.

Do not fear what may happen tomorrow;
The same everlasting Father who cares for you today
will take care of you today and every day.

He will either shield you from suffering
or will give you unfailing strength to bear it.

Be at peace and put aside
all anxious thoughts and imaginations.

Bobby's chemotherapy continued for nine long months. He endured treatments that nearly took his life as a result of the medications, the long-term impact of the prior chemotherapy protocol, and the scarring in his lungs from earlier radiation treatments. While they did not know what tomorrow would bring, Bobby and Dede had a sense of peace because their lives were in God's hands for eternity and they trusted Him. They often wondered how non-believers could navigate through the challenges of life without God.

Finally, they received good news. In May 2009, his cancer was in full remission, but his challenges were not over. Two months later, he was diagnosed with colon cancer which resulted in a colon resection. The doctors were confident they removed all the cancer, and no further treatments were required. Bobby lost a tremendous amount of weight and was weak from surgery, but his faith in God was stronger than ever. Dede did not understand why Bobby had to struggle and suffer through so many ailments and challenges. Thoughts and questions would come into her human mind, but she kept trusting God, and He kept carrying the two of them. Bobby remained cancer free for the rest of his life. Unfortunately, there were more storms to come.

In the fall of 2011, Bobby realized he no longer had the energy and focus he once did. He wanted to ensure his students received the best education possible, so he decided to retire at the end of the school year. In January 2012, Bobby began to feel irregularities in his heart. After several doctor appointments and tests, it became clear that he once again required open heart surgery. Fortunately, they were able to postpone the surgery so Bobby could attend the last high school graduation before his retirement. It was a wonderful, special memory he cherished as his faith-filled journey continued with Dede at his side.

In July 2012, Bobby endured open-heart surgery to replace his aortic and mitral heart valves. The eight-hour surgery was complicated. His weak lungs from the radiation treatments thirty years earlier, combined with other issues, required Bobby to remain in the hospital for the next three months dependent on a ventilator. The doctors tried numerous times to wean him without success. His lungs and body were too weak, leaving him primarily bedridden. His active alert mind was trapped in his exhausted human body. Despite his situation, his faith in God remained strong. He knew God was with him.

As the days, weeks, then months went on, Dede strived to balance her stress and concerns about Bobby combined with her daily responsibilities. She was mentally and physically exhausted. As the alarm went off at 4 AM, Dede pulled herself out of bed, quickly walked the dogs, visited Bobby in the hospital, worked all day as a Vice President in a Fortune 500 company, went home to check on the dogs, then rushed to the hospital to spend quality time in the evening with him, only to collapse in bed so she could be up at 4 AM and start again. Her highlight every day was watching his face light up when she entered his room every morning and evening. She praised God for sustaining their journey together.

They finally moved Bobby to the Specialty Hospital that had expertise in weaning patients from a ventilator. For months, Bobby continued to try to breathe on his own, but he would routinely panic as he gasped for air, trying not to suffocate. He became discouraged as his body continued to wither away; he continued to lean on God and Dede for strength. Bobby and Dede knew his only hope was a miracle.

Then in December 2012, Dede found herself in excruciating pain due to a kidney stone. She suddenly found herself sitting all alone in a hospital gown awaiting surgery. While quietly sitting in the waiting room, two women who were volunteer ministers approached her. When they asked how she was doing, Dede instantly broke down and began to sob for the first time in over five years. Despite her faith, the months and months of Bobby's heart-wrenching illness combined with her pain and pending surgery became too much for her to bear. The wonderful women comforted Dede as she openly shared her situation. The simple act of crying and verbally expressing her feelings provided emotional relief.

As Dede began to compose herself, the women offered a simple yet amazing thought that changed Dede's life forever. As she listened intently, they described the simple, yet powerful "Footprints" poem and asked her to think of her life as a walk down the beach with God. "As you reflect on your life, sometimes there were two sets of footprints in the sand. However, during the difficult times in your life, there was only one set of footprints because God was carrying you during those challenging times." Immediately, Dede felt a sense of peace as she realized God was with her during every trial, adverse medical report, and disappointment. He carried her through the storms and gave her the strength to persevere and press forward. She was amazed and grateful how God provided these two women exactly when her heart needed encouragement and hope. Dede was grateful.

In January, Bobby's physical condition continued to deteriorate as Dede endured her marathon days of support; the doctors had no other medical options to offer. It was at this time that Bobby began the painful decision-making process for his life. Bobby soon asked to speak to a priest as he continued to fully trust God. He wanted to ensure it was acceptable to remove himself from the ventilator. The priest provided great comfort to Bobby by simply stating, "If you take a step in faith to live with God, you do not have to worry about making this decision. If you remove yourself from the ventilator and cannot survive, then it is God's will." After the conversation, Bobby was at peace as he continued to lean on God's promises.

> *"Yea, though I walk through the valley of the shadow of death, I will fear no evil: for thou art with me; thy rod and thy staff they comfort me." Psalm 23:4 (KJV)*

During the following week, Bobby spent precious time with his family. He asked to see a friend with whom he had a long-term disagreement. They were able to reconcile, which brought peace to both of them. At that point, a calmness came over Bobby. It was evident he was in complete harmony with God. For the first time in months, his beautiful blue eyes sparkled once again.

Bobby was now ready to release his life to God. As his family and doctors gathered in the room, he said, "Let's get this show on the road." The doctors carefully removed Bobby from the ventilator and his family remained with him for six peaceful hours. Bobby never had a panic attack. As his breathing became shallow, a priest from the local parish appeared without notice. He laid his hands on Bobby's head, prayed over him, and anointed him. An amazing calm came over Bobby. Shortly afterward, his suffering ended, and he was at peace resting with the Lord.

Hundreds of people joined Dede at Bobby's viewing and funeral. Past students, family, and friends came to pay their respects. She was overwhelmed by the outpouring of love and stories about Bobby as she continued to trust God and lean on Him for strength. A scholarship was established in Bobby's honor.

As she attempted to look forward, her heart was so broken, and her grief was so deep it literally hurt. She found comfort and relief by writing thank you notes, continuing her spiritual readings, and praying to God. Two weeks after the funeral, she returned to work as a positive distraction to keep her mind busy. As time passed, she slowly re-emerged from her grief cocoon and started to live again.

"Blessed are those who mourn, for they will be comforted."
Matthew 5:4 (NIV)

After nearly eighteen months of sadness and grief, an unexpected light appeared in her life. A longtime friend and former co-worker who lived about three hours away called. He reached out to see how she was holding up. She soon found herself laughing and enjoying the phone conversation. It felt good to laugh again. They found themselves talking on the phone for hours at a time. After a few months, he finally asked her to attend a wedding with him. There was an unexpected spark between them. The type of magical spark most people only experience once in their lives.

For the next six months, Dede and Bill enjoyed a long-distance romance which included hours of rich, fun phone conversations. They would frequently meet for one-day dates. Bill loved holding hands on romantic walks. They enjoyed lunches, dinners, laughter about the simple things in life, and their shared love of God. Their relationship was exactly what Dede needed to re-engage in life. As the months went on, they fell in love. God blessed both of them with an unanticipated love that He knitted together. Joy, happiness, and hope filled her heart again.

Then one Saturday night, she called Bill, but he never called back. It was odd, and she made excuses in her mind. The next day, his phone just rang. Then, a dreaded phone call came from his son with the gut-wrenching news. Bill had passed away due to a massive heart attack. He was gone.

Dede was once again devastated. She did not have the energy to move forward on her own and immediately turned to God. She asked Him for the strength to endure. "It was as if He just opened His arms up and embraced me." God once again strengthened, carried, and comforted her as only our Heavenly Father can do.

Dede shared, "Bobby was the love of my life for forty years. I'm not sure why he had to suffer so much. Despite his battles, we chose to live a remarkable, faith-filled journey with God. He strengthened and carried us at every bump in the road of life, even when we did not realize it. God never left us. He sustained us over and over."

Dede continued, "I'm not sure how people navigate through life without the extraordinary hope, strength, and love only God can provide. If you simply trust Him, He will give you all the strength you need each and every day. He will never let you down."

She then added, "God has a plan for everyone's life; knowing this fact helps you get up every morning and keep moving forward. He blessed me with two wonderful men. The unexpected love of Bill re-opened my eyes to life. You have to be open to fulfilling God's purpose for your life even when it hurts. I don't know what lies ahead, but I choose to place my life in His hands and praise Him throughout the journey."

Dede's Favorite Picture From Their Wedding

Dede and Bobby Enjoying Life Together

REFLECTION

1. Many times, we live our lives assuming we, along with our friends and loved ones, will be here tomorrow. As demonstrated in Dede's story, there are no guarantees about our time here on earth.

   Pause and reflect. Are there things you need to say or want to share with someone today? If yes, who do you want to reach out to? What do you want to say or share?

   _____

   _____

   _____

   _____

   _____

   Don't delay. Follow-through on your heart's desires that you wrote down above. Pick up the phone or go see that person now.

2. Prayer is a powerful gift and privilege. Through prayer, we are empowered to seek help, guidance, wisdom, healing, strength, forgiveness, comfort, and peace directly from God. Prayer also provides us with the opportunity to praise and thank God for our many blessings.

   Pause and reflect. Are you engaging God through His gift of prayer? *Yes / No*

   If yes, how and when are you praying?

   _____

   _____

   _____

   _____

   _____

3. Bobby was heartbroken when he thought he lost his ability to pray. He valued and cherished the time he spent with God in prayer.

   Do you value the time you spend in prayer?

   _____

   _____

   _____

   _____

   _____

   _____

   _____

4. Sometimes we are hurting (physically or emotionally) and are not able to find the words to pray. Name at least one person that will pray for you or with you.

   _____

   _____

   _____

   _____

   _____

NEXT STEPS

1. God hears our thoughts and prayers 24/7 — from our short one-sentence prayers to the times when we are on our knees. Unfortunately, many times people say they are just too busy to pray.

   Is there a regular place and time that you can pray? Perhaps before work, in the shower, on a walk, in the car, or right before bed? The key is to find a place and time that works best for you. Where and when can you pray?

   Where: _____

   _____

   When: _____

2. Are you willing to make a commitment to pray every day for the next thirty days? *Yes / No*

_____

_____

_____

_____

CLOSING PRAYER

Our prayers do not need to have fancy words. Just bow your head, close your eyes and talk to God from your heart. Have a conversation with Him. Pause and try it now.

Dear God,

Thank you for the gift and privilege to come to you in prayer. You are amazing and I love you. Please help me with

_____

_____

_____

_____

_____

Thank you for listening to my prayer. Amen.

Rebuilding a Shattered Life

"He heals the brokenhearted and binds up their wounds."
Psalm 147:3 (NIV)

"God, God, help me, help me...I'm losing my mind!" Suzie cried out as she threw her phone across the room, flung the door open, and ran outside. "God, I beg you to help me." Suzie, now twenty-five, was experiencing the horrific flashbacks of being raped, something she had successfully blocked for years. The pictures in her mind started without warning and were becoming more frequent and graphic. For a solid week, the flashbacks haunted her over and over again. She thought she was losing her mind. The images in her head were sickening and grotesque; she could not turn them off. When she finally reached the end of her ability to cope, she called a suicide hotline where she was placed on hold.

As Suzie panicked and ran into the yard, she looked up to heaven and cried out, "God help me!" Immediately, she felt the cool cleansing rain splashing the tears of horror away from her face. She could feel God's calming love surrounding her as she began to breathe again. Suzie was broken, full of fear, and beyond despair, but God heard her cries for help that day. At that moment, He reached down from heaven, met her in a broken state, and embraced her with His peace and love. When Suzie once again lifted her eyes toward heaven, she saw a bright, breathtaking, and brilliant rainbow. She knew God was with her. She then paused and remembered God's promises that she learned as a child from her grandmother. From that point forward, her healing process began with God at her side.

Suzie's painful story began at age twelve. She was raped by a stranger while playing in a fort she built with her friends in the desert. Suzie never told her parents about the attack. If she had only obeyed her parents and not "snuck out" of her bedroom window that night to play in the fort, this terrible incident would not have occurred. Suzie believed the attack was her fault and she was a bad person. She blocked the violent event and moved forward.

About a month later, Suzie awoke to one of her parent's drunk adult friends making unwanted advances toward her. She was able to fight him off and report the incident the next day. When her daddy heard about the attack, he became extremely violent toward the man. Her mom, on the other hand, blamed Suzie for upsetting her dad. A few days later, as her mom drove her to school, she confronted Suzie and directly asked her, "Did you provoke the incident?" Suzie said nothing. As soon as she arrived at school, this young girl found a dictionary to look up the word "provoked" – she did not know what it meant. She decided she must be a terrible person and there must be something wrong with her. Her self-esteem was shattered, and she began to misbehave.

At age thirteen, Suzie's step-brother began to molest and rape her. She was petrified. She did not know what to do. She feared if she reported the attacks, her dad would become violent once again and possibly kill her step-brother while her mom would blame her for everything. So, Suzie remained silent and began to block the horrendous advances out of her mind. She turned to alcohol and drugs to suppress her thoughts. By age fifteen, the regular attacks stopped when her step-brother moved out of the house, but the damage was done.

Suzie, now a sophomore, was failing high school. Her favorite morning drink before school was orange juice and vodka. She began using whatever drugs she could get her hands on to block her thoughts including marijuana, cocaine, mushrooms, acid, and speed. Her heart was hard, she was tough as nails, and she had no compassion for anyone. She was out of control.

At age seventeen, during her junior year in high school, Suzie was rushed to the hospital in severe pain. She had a large cyst which resulted in a partial hysterectomy. After the surgery, her life continued to spiral out of control due to her use of alcohol and drugs. At age nineteen, she was living with her fiancé, a drug dealer who was mentally abusive. He isolated her from friends and family while destroying any self-esteem that remained.

As she did her best to exist day after day, her medical issues resurfaced. She began to experience severe abdominal pain once again. This time, however, Suzie was blessed to have a wonderful doctor that cared about her as a whole person, not just her medical issues. Unfortunately, he quickly discovered she had a uterine cyst the size of a grapefruit. If they were unable to stop the rapidly growing cyst, she would require a full hysterectomy. To make matters worse, as a result of medical tests, she learned her fiancé had recently transmitted chlamydia to her, which meant he was cheating with other women. She was angry, afraid, and overwhelmed with pain, both physically and emotionally.

For the next several weeks, her doctor worked to save her ability to have children as he also focused on rebuilding her self-esteem and self-worth. He emphasized that she was a wonderful young woman and a good person – words she had never heard before. Her doctor began to explain there was more to life than what she had settled for. He helped Suzie to see what she deserved in a man. He became a role model for the type of man she wanted in her life.

During this same time, her fiancé's abuse escalated, and he physically hit her. However, due to the kind words and encouragement she received from her doctor, Suzie realized she deserved more out of life. She kicked her fiancé out of the house and changed the locks. She finally grasped that God had a better life planned for her, but had no idea where to go from there or how to pursue an improved way of life; she had no support system.

A few weeks later, her cyst became infected, and her fever spiked to 104 degrees. As her doctor held her hand, tears rolled down his face as he said, "I'm sorry, but I must do a complete hysterectomy to save your life." Her opportunity to have children was gone at age nineteen, but strangely, her self-assurance started to improve. Perhaps there was hope.

Six months later, Suzie had an intestinal blockage that nearly killed her. When she finally regained consciousness and opened her eyes, she saw a nurse praying over her. The fact that a nurse would take the time to pray for a stranger deeply touched her heart. Suzie realized she needed a change in her life. She soon gathered her limited belongings and moved to another city about four hours away for a fresh start. Unfortunately, she quickly fell back into her old pattern of life. For the next six years, she continued to party and successfully block her past. Then, the horrific flashbacks started. However, through it all, she continued to remember a Bible verse that her grandmother taught her as a child:

"For God so loved the world, that he gave his only begotten Son, that whosoever believeth in Him shall not perish, but have everlasting life." John 3:16 (KJV)

Due to the severity of her flashbacks and situation, Suzie finally obtained the professional help that she desperately needed. Through extensive counseling and a friend that invited her to church, Suzie's world began to reshape over the next few years. She started to deal with the pain and memories she had successfully suppressed. Then, she slowly stopped relying on drugs and alcohol as she began to trust and rely on God.

As time progressed, Suzie began to read the Bible and participate in Bible studies through the mail, and then in small Bible study groups. She started to notice that God was filling a massive hole in her heart as prayer became a key component of her daily routine. Her self-esteem began to improve, and she felt better about herself. During her long recovery journey, she found refuge in the following Bible verses:

"So do not fear, for I am with you; do not be dismayed, for I am your God. I will strengthen you and help you; I will uphold you with my righteous right hand."
Isaiah 41:10 (NIV)

"Peace I leave with you; my peace I give you. I do not give to you as the world gives. Do not let your hearts be troubled and do not be afraid." John 14:27 (NIV)

Then, the day of freedom finally came. Suzie let go of her past and fully trusted God. She prayed a simple prayer as she offered her broken life to her Heavenly Father. Suzie had nothing else to give Him. Through her acceptance of Jesus into her heart, she was able to begin the journey of rebuilding and forgiveness. As she started her long forgiveness process, she found comfort in the following Bible verses:

"Forget the former things; do not dwell on the past."
Isaiah 43:18 (NIV)

"Get rid of all bitterness, rage and anger, brawling and slander, along with every form of malice. Be kind and compassionate to one another, forgiving each other, just as in Christ God forgave you." Ephesians 4: 31-32 (NIV)

Several years have now passed. Suzie is enjoying a Christ-filled life, set free from alcohol and drugs as well as the horrific flashbacks of things she endured at an early age. She has been married to a loving and caring man for over twenty years. He treats her with the respect and dignity that her doctor described several years earlier. Suzie reflected, "Due to my past pain and suffering, I am now able to sense and notice when people are hurting. I have a new level of compassion for others. I know there is still work that needs to be done in me but praise God–I am a broken vessel willing to be used for God's glory." With God's help, she not only forgave her step-brother but faithfully reached out to him when he was in need. She also forgave her mom and cared for her on a daily basis during her last stages of cancer.

In closing, Suzie shared, "The painful events of my life are now a distant past. God can re-mold everyone's lives for good. If your life resembles a chipped, cracked, or shattered pot, our loving God is an amazing potter. He can remold and piece your life back together into something wonderful. He can and will use your life story to help rescue others from their shattered worlds and bring them into the warm light of the Lord. There is hope, healing, and life with God – Real Life! Nothing can compare. Praise God!"

REFLECTION

1. Pause and Reflect. Do you struggle with current or past events in your life? *Yes / No*

   If yes, what are they?

   _____

   _____

   _____

   _____

   _____

   _____

   _____

2. Do you need to seek professional support to work through your past situations? *Yes / No*

3. If yes, below are few resources where you can ask for help.

   Your Doctor   Your Counselor   Hot Lines

   Your Pastor   Employee Assistance Program   County Services

   Other Resources: _____

   _____

   _____

   _____

   _____

   _____

   _____

NEXT STEPS

1. God loves you no matter what has happened to you or what you have done in your past. Do you believe this? *Yes / No*
Write down your thoughts.

_____

_____

_____

_____

2. Do you want to ask God to help you move forward with your life? *Yes / No*

3. If you answered yes, what do you want to ask Him?

_____

_____

_____

_____

_____

CLOSING PRAYER

Dear Heavenly Father,

Thank you for loving me no matter what has happened in my past. Please help me to overcome my past situations and give me the courage to seek professional support as required. Please help me to move forward with my life. I need help with _____.
Thank you for caring about me and loving me! Amen.

Overcoming a Broken Heart

*"My flesh and my heart may fail, but God is the strength
of my heart and my portion forever." Psalm 73:26*

Beth fell to her knees and sobbed. Her hopes and dreams of having a baby were crushed once again as she miscarried for the sixth time. While she tried to compose herself, and catch her breath, she quietly prayed, "God, will you ever bless me with a child?" Beth knew God forgave her for a decision she made over twenty years earlier but kept wondering if the miscarriages were a punishment for her sins. Her heart was broken.

Beth was raised in a traditional, loving, and strict Christian home. As she navigated through her teenage years, she began to explore new areas and ventured beyond the boundaries she learned in church and from her family. During her senior year of high school, the relationship with her boyfriend became more involved, and they were intimate for several months. Before departing for college, they decided to break off their relationship. They were not in love, and it was time to move on. Then, while away from home during her first semester of college, Beth received the shock of her life. She was pregnant.

Based on her family's beliefs, Beth was afraid, ashamed, and embarrassed to tell her parents about the pregnancy. Disappointing her parents, especially her father, was not an option she wanted to explore. She also harbored a profound fear her family would completely reject her once they heard her news. Beth shared, "My self-confidence was low, I was by myself, and I panicked."

Subsequently, Beth made the decision to protect her family and herself. She never told her parents about the pregnancy. Her decision obviously removed any possibility of carrying her baby to full term and pursuing adoption options. She numbed herself to her relationship with God and allowed her human-side to take over. Beth made the difficult decision to pursue an abortion.

With the help of her roommate's mother, Beth found a doctor who performed a second-trimester abortion. Beth shared, "At age nineteen, I failed to completely comprehend the magnitude of my decision. My primary focus was to put this situation behind me, move forward with my college education, and keep my reputation intact."

The day of the abortion was somber. She was grateful for the nurse who held her hand as the pregnancy was terminated. After the abortion, she looked at the doctor and asked if the procedure was completely confidential. The doctor responded, "No, I'm going to put an ad in the paper." His cold tone and comment pierced her heart. From that point, Beth mentally blocked the abortion from her mind and moved forward with her life, or so she thought.

Over the next ten years, Beth graduated from college and pursued an exciting career. From the outside looking in, she had it all. She was an attractive woman with an active social life. She enjoyed wearing the latest designer styles, interacting with senior executives, and hobnobbing at the city's trendy restaurants. However, despite her successful, exciting, and glamorous life, something was missing.

Beth found herself jumping from relationship to relationship while she silently struggled with low self-confidence. She desperately wanted to find someone who loved her. Unfortunately, she was repeatedly attracted to men with strong and big personalities, on the spectrum of narcissists. Men who kept her on edge as they fed their egos and played mind games at the detriment of her self-esteem. Beth was caught in a vicious cycle and felt unworthy of love. She relied on men to validate her self-worth versus looking to God.

At age twenty-nine, most of her friends were now married or engaged. Her confidence hit a new low as she pondered what was next. Was this all life had to offer? One day while visiting friends, she happened to pick up an old magazine to pass the time. As she began to flip through the pages, an advertisement caught her eye. The heading read, "Would you like to have a personal relationship with Jesus?" The article perked her interest. As she read the commentary, it deeply touched her heart, as if God was speaking to her directly. At that moment, Beth knew she wanted Jesus back in her life. But, how was it going to happen given her past decisions? She felt unworthy of His love.

For the next six months, Beth began a deep, soul-searching journey as she read the Bible, attended church, and started to pray again. She was keenly aware life on her own, separated from God, was not working. She was tired of being sad and lonely as she relied on men to fill the void in her heart and diminish her emotional scars from ten years earlier. Beth no longer wanted to live in the shadow of the abortion or her past. The guilt was a burden she could no longer carry on her own.

Finally, Beth chose to be completely transparent with God and confess her sins. She admitted failing to follow His commandments and asked for forgiveness. She specifically confessed her abortion and how sorry she was for her decision. Beth wanted to pursue a new life centered around a relationship with Jesus as her personal Savior, without the baggage from her past life. God lovingly embraced Beth at that moment, just the way she was.

*"Repent, then, and turn to God, so that your
sins may be wiped out, that times of refreshing
may come from the Lord." Acts 3:19 (NIV)*

For the next six years, love, commitment, and marriage continued to elude Beth as she faithfully asked God to bless her with a Christian husband. She continued to trust God and wait on His timing. Then, a surprising thing happened. She entered into a relationship with a friend she had known for nearly ten years. Don was unlike any man she previously dated. He was patient, kind, and tried to put her feelings first. Obviously, God had a plan. After a short engagement, they were married. They wanted to start a family quickly since Beth was now thirty-seven and her biological clock was ticking.

They were thrilled when Beth learned she was pregnant. As their minds began to explode with hopes and aspirations for their unborn child, their dreams came to an abrupt ending when she miscarried. Beth was devastated as she conceptually realized sometimes this happens. However, she harbored a powerful, guilty feeling she was being punished for the abortion, eighteen years earlier.

Beth intellectually knew she was forgiven for the abortion and her past sins, but there was an element of brokenness in her heart. She was unable to forgive herself and carried the heavy burden on a daily basis. Beth struggled and believed she did not deserve to have a baby. In retrospect, she now realizes had she turned her burden and feelings over to God, she would have avoided six years of torture.

*"For as high as the heavens are above the earth, so
great is his love for those who fear him; as far as
the east is from the west, so far has he removed our
transgressions from us." Psalm 103:11-12 (NIV)*

Within a few months, Beth was pregnant once again. As the weeks progressed, their apprehensive excitement grew. Then, once again, a devastating reality hit. She miscarried a second time, followed by a third, and fourth miscarriage. Beth was on an emotional roller coaster as she became obsessed with having a baby. It consumed her thoughts morning, noon, and night. On many days, she was so preoccupied begging God for a child, she failed to pause and seek His direction. Through the rough years, Don did his best to support Beth during their painful journey.

"The Lord is close to the brokenhearted and saves those who are crushed in spirit." Psalm 34:18 (NIV)

Due to financial constraints, they were unable to pursue fertility options. This angered Beth and caused friction at home. Finally, when her quest to have a baby seemed impossible, she completely surrendered her hopes and dreams to be a mother and placed them in God's hands. From that point forward, Beth's desires transitioned into a personal journey with God, unlike anything she had ever experienced. She knew the creator and father of life, was the only one who could bless her with a child.

"Be still, and know that I am God." Psalm 46:10 (NIV)

As Beth leaned on God for emotional strength, a level of peace and calmness began to surround her. He started to encircle her with amazing, Christian women who provided support and prayers during the remainder of her painful journey. She embraced their support and God's unconditional love as she suffered through a fifth and then a sixth miscarriage.

After her sixth miscarriage, they began an adoption process. A few months later, Beth learned she was pregnant once again. She was emotionally drained as her doctor performed a weekly ultrasound due to her high-risk pregnancy, but this time her pregnancy felt different. At week thirteen, Beth's doctor stopped the weekly ultrasound procedures and continued to carefully monitor her pregnancy. A few weeks later, Beth and Don stopped the adoption process as they placed all their energy and hope into her pregnancy.

A level of apprehensive excitement began to grow as Beth progressed to sixteen weeks, then twenty and twenty-four weeks of her pregnancy. She kept trusting God, but quietly feared every doctor appointment. Then, during her last trimester, she began to experience symptoms which indicated a premature delivery. Beth held tightly to her faith in God as she was confined to bed rest for the last two months of her pregnancy.

Finally, at 3:48 AM on an extraordinary day, joy and thanksgiving filled a delivery room as she heard the doctor say, "It's a boy!" Tears of joy ran down her face as she held Cameron for the first time. At age forty-two, after six miscarriages and five years since their marriage, Beth's prayers were answered. They were the proud parents of a healthy baby boy. God, the powerful father of life, had blessed her.

At Cameron's baptism, Beth was overwhelmed with a grateful heart as she sobbed and held her gift from God. She shared "God was with me every step of my journey and carried me through deep valleys and heartbreaks. I will forever be thankful."

Over the next five years, Beth and Don cherished the opportunity to be parents as they dreamed of a little brother or sister for Cameron. Unfortunately, they suffered the heartbreak of two additional miscarriages. After deep conversations, they decided to pursue a non-domestic adoption and set the wheels in motion. Since their family would be expanding once again, they purchased a new home and prepared for their baby's arrival. As the adoption date drew near and the excitement grew, they purchased airline tickets and made final arrangements to bring their baby home. Everything was set.

The night before their flight, they received a phone message from the adoption agency asking them to call early the next morning. No other information was offered. They were immediately filled with fear and prayed. The next morning, Beth began praying when she opened her eyes. She begged God to ensure there were no issues with the adoption. Unfortunately, when Don placed the call, they were informed the adoption had fallen through. The baby's mother decided to keep her baby at the last minute. They were heartbroken.

Over the next few months, Beth and Don came to terms with their disappointments and decided to no longer pursue future adoptions. They did not understand why they had to experience the pain of the last minute failed adoption, but they know God was with them. He does not always answer our prayers, but He loves us unconditionally and knows what is best for us.

In closing, Beth shared, "Our God is amazing. As a result of grace and the gift of Jesus, I am able to move forward through life, finally at peace. In retrospect, the emotional pain I experienced through eight miscarriages and a failed adoption strengthened my relationship with God. He was in the storms with me and never left my side, even when I tried to ignore him. Through His strength, I am now able to share my story. I pray it will touch the lives of others in need. I believe every conception has a soul and I know all my little kids are safe in the arms of Jesus. I look forward to an amazing reunion in heaven."

REFLECTION

1. Past decisions and actions can leave painful, emotional scars. Satan takes advantage of our scars to control us through feelings of guilt and shame. He strives to keep us away from the light of God's love by making us feel unworthy, but there is good news! No matter what we have done, if we confess our mistakes and ask for forgiveness, God erases our sins as we strive to do what is right in the eyes of the Lord:

   "If we confess our sins, he is faithful and just and will forgive us our sins and purify us from all unrighteousness." 1 John 1:9 (NIV)

2. Sometimes after God forgives us, we fail to forgive ourselves and continue to carry our burdens. Do you need to forgive yourself for your past mistakes? *Yes / No*

   If you answered yes, then pray this prayer:

   Dear God,

   I know I have confessed _____ to you. Thank you for forgiving me. Unfortunately, I continue to feel guilty and punish myself for _____. Will you please help me to forgive myself and release my anxiety to you? Thank you. Amen.

3. For years, Beth searched for love and happiness. Do you feel you have a void in your life? *Yes / No* If you answered yes, what are you searching for?

   _____

   _____

   _____

   _____

Pause and share the void you described with God. He is waiting to listen to you. Ask for His guidance and direction.

NEXT STEPS

1. As we learned from Beth's story, sometimes we are so busy talking to God and asking him for things, we fail to pause and listen to Him. Find a quiet place where you will not be disturbed for the next five minutes. Sit down and get comfortable. Close your eyes and take three slow, deep breaths. Relax your facial muscles and drop your shoulders. Now pray this prayer and sit quietly.

   Dear God,

   I get entwined with my busy days as I try to accomplish things on my own. I know I fail to pause and listen for your voice and guidance. Please forgive me. As I quietly sit here with you, please search my heart and reveal what you want me to know today. I love you and trust you. Thank you. Amen.

2. What did you learn in the last five minutes?

   _____

   _____

   _____

   _____

   _____

   _____

   _____

CLOSING PRAYER

Dear God,

Thank you for loving me despite my errors, mistakes, and flaws. Please guide and direct me as I move forward. I love you. Amen.

When the Storms Keep Coming

"And the peace of God, which transcends all understanding, will guard your hearts and your minds in Christ Jesus." Philippians 4:7 (NIV)

There are dark things that happen in our fallen world. The story below contains a sampling of the frightening and disturbing incidents a family endured, but there is good news. Through the power of prayer, God triumphs once again. As you read through some of the events, remember God loves you unconditionally. If you simply ask, He will be with you when you walk through the valleys and storms of your life. He is powerful!

Crystal was petrified as she prayed for God's guidance and strength. She did her best to hold back her tears and concentrate as she signed the final papers to admit her daughter into a confined psychiatric hospital. Due to her fragile suicidal condition, her youngest daughter Bridget required round-the-clock monitoring and psychiatric care in a structured environment. Crystal was so grateful that God had intervened and opened her eyes so she could see the hurting heart of her daughter before it was too late.

Crystal's family challenges began seven years earlier. She was a very involved and loving mother. Bill was a quiet, devoted husband and father, and their two girls, Rebecca and Bridget were happy, fun children. Life was great. Then odd problems began to surface around their home such as a tree falling on their fence, house shingles blowing away, a fly infiltration in their home, numerous health challenges with their dogs, and a flea infestation despite their clean home. New, odd obstacles appeared nearly weekly. They did their best to make light of the situation with friends and coworkers, but it was noticeable and disturbing.

Due to their faith in God, they started praying and asking for guidance to resolve the weekly events. They were amazed to watch how God resolved issues over a week or a few months. Sometimes the problems just quietly disappeared. They called their answers to prayer "God Instances" and always thanked Him. In retrospect, the minor challenges they endured prepared and strengthened them for a journey no one could have anticipated.

As time went on, the family's obstacles started to escalate to include lost jobs, car accidents, leg injuries, and a major water main break that resulted in a significant financial setback. One night they were tired and decided to skip their nightly laundry and complete it the next day. Due to their change in routine, they were awake the following morning when sparks and large flames started spewing from the dryer as a result of a burning motor. The fire department said their home had been spared as a direct result of their change in routine. Together the family thanked and praised God for keeping them safe.

Crystal and Bill did their best to reassure their daughters that things were OK, but they both quietly questioned if the family was doing something wrong or if they needed to make some changes. They understood that sometimes bad things happen to good people, but it was not normal for so many odd things to be happening. There were days Crystal would get in the car by herself and cry on the way to work. On the days when she no longer had words to pray, she would listen to praise and worship music on the radio for comfort. She leaned heavily on an oasis of friends that provided her with love and support. Despite it all, the family continued to trust God. They prayed for comfort and guidance as they embraced His promises.

"So do not fear, for I am with you; do not be dismayed,
for I am your God. I will strengthen you and help you;
I will uphold you with my righteous right hand."
Isaiah 41:10 (NIV)

The months went on, and the obstacles kept coming like clockwork. Coworkers, friends and family, both believers in God and non-believers, would jokingly ask what problems had surfaced that week. Bill and Crystal would smile, openly share the latest challenges, and then discuss how God was guiding and helping them resolve their current issues. They chose to shine a light on their troubling obstacles instead of living in the shadows of fear. They believed God could and would transform their obstacles into good.

"Be strong and courageous. Do not be afraid or terrified
because of them, for the Lord your God goes with you;
he will never leave you nor forsake you."
Deuteronomy 31:6 (NIV)

Then, Crystal suffered a severe back injury due to a freak accident at work which resulted in chronic pain for the next two years. It impacted her ability to hold a job and handle simple chores around the house. Next, she fell down a flight of stairs injuring a knee and both ankles. They could not explain what was happening or why, but their faith in the Lord was growing stronger and stronger with every obstacle. God was carrying them through life despite their storms. They continued to lean on God for strength and peace, refusing to allow Satan to discourage them.

"For I am the Lord your God who takes hold of your
right hand and says to you, Do not fear; I will help you."
Isaiah 41:13 (NIV)

Unfortunately, during this stressful time, their sweet, youngest daughter Bridget entered high school and began hanging out with a group of friends who were not healthy for her. Over time, Bridget's loving demeanor changed, and she became angry most of the time, but there was no sign of alcohol or drugs. Her parents assumed she was going through the typical teenage years and did not over-think the situation. They thought her attitude would improve as the years moved forward. They had no idea of the scary things that were starting to go on in her life and her mind.

Then one night, Crystal was sound asleep. Suddenly, she sat straight up in bed and began gasping for air. Her heart was pounding as she attempted to orient herself. As her mind began to clear, she realized her terrifying and graphic experience was a dream, but it seemed so real. She vividly saw Bridget calmly step off a street median right into the path of an oncoming car. She witnessed the impact. It was horrific. Why would she have such a dreadful and horrendous dream? Crystal burst into tears and immediately started praying like she had never prayed before. She realized God was providing a warning; her daughter was in danger, but she was unclear of what was going on or what to do next. She began to watch Bridget like a hawk and do what she could to keep her safe as she continued to pray.

During this same time, Bridget started cutting herself, a practice where she intentionally cut and injured her skin without trying to commit suicide. Her friends knew about the cutting, but they did not inform her parents. Then, one of Bridget's friends came across an online blog where Bridget posted many pictures of suicide and described her plan to take her own life by walking in front of a car. Her friend panicked and made Bridget share the shocking information about her cutting and suicide plans with her parents. Crystal and Bill were frightened, horrified, and completely blindsided.

As Crystal began to read Bridget's own words in the blog, a bone-chilling shock transcended throughout her body. The words described in detail the terrifying, graphic dream she had experienced only a few weeks earlier. Then, a sudden jolt of reality set-in. God had intervened and revealed Bridget's hurting heart and suicide plan. He shined a light into Bridget's dark world. God answered their prayers to protect Bridget. They now needed to obtain the professional help she desperately required.

"The light shines in the darkness, and the darkness has not overcome it." John 1:5 (NIV)

Bill and Crystal immediately jumped into action. Crystal called numerous individual psychiatric practices, but no appointments were available. She was frantic as she prayed to God and asked for help. While they worked to remain with Bridget all day and night to keep her safe, Crystal looked for an available bed in a psychiatric hospital or ward. Everything was full.

Suddenly, calmness and peace came over her. She realized they were approaching the situation backward. They should contact a large psychiatric practice to increase their chances of getting an appointment. Crystal quickly identified a practice online and placed a call. Surprisingly, a cancellation had just occurred; they could see Bridget immediately, but there was more. The appointment was made with a psychiatrist who worked at the local psychiatric hospital in the ward for youth. Due to the doctor's connections, she was able to get Bridget the last bed in the hospital. This was not a coincidence. It was apparent God had intervened once again.

Bridget was relieved when she was admitted to the hospital. She felt somewhat liberated to have the pressures of the outside world removed and to know she was finally getting the help she desperately needed. Her parents did their best to reassure her and emphasize that she was not alone. God was with her, and many people were praying for her full recovery. After seven long days and nights, Bridget was discharged from the hospital. The doctors identified her root issues and prescribed medication to begin counteracting her depression. She continued to participate in a daily, highly structured outpatient program that allowed her to spend evenings at home with her family.

At first, it was a slow recovery process. Bridget's anger emerged more and more after she left the hospital. She continued to work with therapists to address her identified issues which also included anorexia tendencies. Her parents did everything in their power to help her. Despite Bridget's desires and efforts to get better, she kept sliding in and out of the recovery process. Her self-esteem was low, and she was very vulnerable.

> *"Be alert and of sober mind. Your enemy the devil prowls around like a roaring lion looking for someone to devour."*
> *1 Peter 5:8 (NIV)*

Then, Bridget entered into an unhealthy dating relationship. It was during this time, she became sullen as her anger intensified and her demeanor became very dark. Bridget wore black clothes, and her hair covered her eyes; the color of her pretty blue eyes transitioned to a dark, almost black color. Despite numerous attempts and approaches to talk and reach out to her, she kept slipping further and further away from her family, her therapists, and her faith in God. It was as if the adversary was stealing her away right in front of their eyes.

> *"Put on the full armor of God, so that you can take your stand against the devil's schemes." Ephesians 6:11 (NIV)*

Finally, after months of intervention and prayer, her dark demeanor started to dissipate as her anger began to disappear. She gradually realized her parents were truly on her side. There was hope!

"The Lord will rescue me from every evil attack and will bring me safely to his heavenly kingdom. To him be glory for ever and ever. Amen." 2 Timothy 4:18 (NIV)

As Bridget slowly started to re-engage in life, she continued to work hard with her therapist to confront her challenges. It was tough when they adjusted medications to balance her mood swings, but she knew it was necessary and she wanted to get better. There were times she would slip back and start cutting again, but as the months passed by, she became healthier and healthier.

As her healing progressed, she began sewing and drawing again. She had fun making bracelets and taking care of animals. Through therapy, Bridget improved how she interacted with her friends, and it felt good. She once again actively participated in the drama department at the high school and was happy to be appreciated for her contributions. The shows and plays provided her with a positive diversion from the challenges in her life. Her faith in God was slowly restored as she realized He was with her during the entire three-year journey. Her blue eyes finally returned. About a year later, Bridget was able to help a friend who attempted suicide and share her faith in God. She found purpose in her life.

As Bridget finally had her feet back on solid ground, the obstacles in their family's life continued. Bill and Crystal faced the challenge of dealing with aging parents. Then, Bridget was diagnosed with postural orthostatic tachycardia syndrome (POTS), which affects the autonomic functions of the body. Bridget was now dealing with the automatic systems in her body functioning irregularly such as her heart rate, blood pressure, digestion, blood flow, body temperature, and others. Despite her latest challenges, Bridget persevered due to her faith in God and her parents that were by her side. She kept moving forward.

Then, their oldest daughter Rebecca fell and hit her head resulting in a severe concussion. The side effects plagued her entire first year of college. This was followed by a year of severe anxiety, some poor choices with boyfriends, and a car accident in which her car was totaled. Crystal went through a lymphoma health scare, but thankfully received a clear bill of health after a few months when the symptoms just disappeared. Bill, on the other hand, was diagnosed with cancer that required a six-hour surgery. The first prognosis required both chemo and radiation. The doctors were shocked after the surgery when the test results revealed all his lymph nodes were clean and no further treatment was required. The family knew there was no such thing as a coincidence. God was working overtime to transform evil into good.

> *"And we know that in all things God works for the good of those who love him, who have been called according to his purpose." Romans 8:28 (NIV)*

It is difficult to understand why Crystal's family has been plagued by so many obstacles. However, their response to their on-going challenges has been a testimony to believers and non-believers close by and far away. Numerous co-workers, friends, and neighbors have been amazed as they have personally witnessed God's guidance, love, and support during their many storms.

Crystal shared, "It is amazing to fully trust God and watch His power unfold. On my lowest days, he gave me peace in the middle of our storms. He provided exactly what we needed when we required it through people, finances, doctors, a song on the radio, or words of encouragement from a friend. When any little victory happened, or positive news was received, no matter how small, I would praise God like crazy and thank him for his help."

Crystal continued, "We live in a fallen world. Satan seeks to kill, steal, and destroy, but we have good news! God continues to help us overcome our obstacles. We grow closer to Him with every new challenge. "

"When you face serious issues such as the possible death of your child, every day with that child is a huge blessing, no matter what other challenges are going on in your life. I hope and pray the constant obstacles stop, but if they don't, I'm thankful to have God on this journey with us."

> "...In this world, you will have trouble. But take heart!
> I have overcome the world." John 16:33 (NIV)

REFLECTION

As we saw in this family's story, sometimes challenges and obstacles keep coming our way. Remember, Satan wants us to live in the shadows of fear, embarrassment, chaos, and exhaustion where he has control over our lives. He wants us to live in darkness.

There is Good News and Hope! God loves you! Do not be afraid. Reach out and ask God for His help with your challenges and obstacles. He is waiting to help you!

1. Are you currently facing obstacles or challenges in your life that are overwhelming, intimidating, or frightening? If yes, list those obstacles below.

_____

_____

_____

_____

_____

_____

_____

2. Pause and reflect. Why are you feeling overwhelmed, intimidated, or frightened?

_____

_____

_____

_____

_____

_____

_____

WHEN THE STORMS KEEP COMING

3. Have you stopped and asked God for help or guidance? *Yes / No*

   If you answered no, what guidance would you want from God?

   _____

   _____

   _____

   _____

   _____

   _____

   _____

   _____

   _____

NEXT STEPS

1. Find a quiet place and spend a few minutes with God. Pray this simple prayer:

   Dear God,

   Thank you for loving me. I need your help to move forward. Specifically, I need help with _____ so that I can _____. Please guide and direct me as I step forward in faith under your umbrella of love, grace, and power. Give me strength and peace as I face my obstacles and challenges with you. Thank you in advance for helping me. You are an awesome God. Amen.

2. Sit still for a moment. With God's help, what positive steps or actions can you take to tackle your current obstacles?

   Some potential ideas might include:

   • Continuing to pray—Ask God for specific guidance and direction

   • Reaching out to a friend, family member, pastor, or counselor and asking for help

- Searching the internet for Bible verses regarding your situation, then memorizing one or two of the verses

- Taking one small action to overcome your obstacles to build positive momentum

_____

_____

_____

_____

_____

3. Do you know someone who is struggling with a current obstacle or challenge in their life? If yes, list the person's name below. Now, ask God how He can use you to help that person. Listen as God speaks to your heart.

_____

_____

_____

_____

_____

CLOSING PRAYER

Dear God,

Thank you for your guidance, wisdom, and strength. Please be with me as I step out in faith to tackle my latest challenges. It is such a comfort to know you are with me in the midst of my personal storms. I love you. Amen.

Seeking God's Direction – Your Story

*"Can any one of you by worrying add a
single hour to your life?" Matthew 6:27 (NIV)*

As I was writing this book, it became clear that the last chapter should be about your story. So, let's write this interactive chapter together as you seek God's direction in your life.

It was another challenging night and it was difficult to sleep. I was once again worried about:

- _____
  _____
  _____

- _____
  _____
  _____

- _____
  _____
  _____

As I tossed and turned, I thought. "I can't sleep. I need to get up for work in the morning. What am I going to do?" Then, I had this interesting thought. "God is available 24/7 and He will always listen to me." As I rolled over again and adjusted my pillow, I took a deep breath, closed my eyes, and began to talk to God as my best friend. I simply discussed my worries and concerns from my heart – no fancy talk or special words. I was completely open and honest. And then I paused and said, "I can't do this alone anymore. Please help me with the following:

- _____
  _____

- _____
  _____

- _____
  _____

As I closed my prayer, I asked God for his guidance, direction, and peace regarding the next steps I should take. When I said "Amen," I paused and took a slow, deep breath. I could literally feel my anxiety diminish as the tenseness in my chest lifted away. "WOW," I thought. "Is it really that simple?" I knew I would not get an instant resolution to my requests, but it was comforting to know that God, the creator of the universe, was on my side.

Over the next few days, I started to pay attention to my thoughts. When I began to worry, I stopped and remembered God was in control. Then, I asked myself, "What benefit am I receiving from the hours and hours that I spend worrying." So, I decided to sit down and write down all the positive things that happened as a result of my worrying:

1. _____

_____

2. _____

_____

3. _____

_____

When I realized my list was BLANK, it dawned on me that worry was an empty, non-value activity. It was Satan's way of keeping me preoccupied, distracted, and miserable. I then remembered a few Bible verses that quickly re-centered me:

"Yes, my soul, find rest in God; my hope comes from him. Truly he is my rock and my salvation; he is my fortress, I will not be shaken." Psalm 62:5-6 (NIV)

"Do not be anxious about anything, but in every situation, by prayer and petition, with thanksgiving, present your requests to God. And the peace of God, which transcends all understanding, will guard your hearts and your minds in Christ Jesus." Philippians 4:6-7 (NIV)

"When I am afraid, I put my trust in you." Psalm 56:3 (NIV)

I know my journey is on-going, but I take great comfort in knowing, "...If God is for us, who can be against us." Romans 8:31 (NIV)

Closing Thoughts

The simple truth...God loves us!

We are His children, and He is our Heavenly Father! He will carry us through life's storms if we will simply stop and ask Him for guidance and strength! Even in the valleys of our lives, there are always rainbows. Look up to God for your direction, joy, and encouragement. Keep your eyes focused on Him and His purpose for your life. Open your heart to His unconditional love and keep your faith entrenched in his promises.

> *"But seek first his kingdom and his righteousness..."*
> *Matthew 6:33 (NIV)*

Remember God is always with us. He is always with YOU! Praise God!!

Three Steps to Salvation

If you are interested in real victory –
a personal relationship with God,
follow the steps below.

1. Get Ready...

Admit you have sinned. Tell God what you have done, be sorry for it, and be willing to quit.

> *"For all have sinned and fall short of the glory of God."*
> *Romans 3:23 (NIV)*

2. Get Set...

Believe God loves you and sent His Son, Jesus, to save you from your sins. Accept the forgiveness God offers you.

> *"For God so loved the world that he gave his one and only Son, that whoever believes in Him shall not perish, but have eternal life." John 3:16 (NIV)*

3. Go!

Claim Jesus as your Savior. Acknowledge God's forgiveness, respond with love, and follow Jesus.

> *"Everyone who calls on the name of the Lord will be saved." Romans 10:13 (NIV)*

Share your victory with a friend as you begin your new journey.

http://nazarene.org/ministries/ssm/children/programs/vbs/steps/display.html

Lessons Learned While Writing This Book

In the summer of 2015, the Lord told me to write a book focused on overcoming the tragedies and hardships in life. I consciously dismissed the Lord's voice on numerous occasions. I didn't want to write on that topic. I had planned to write a book on leadership and already had it outlined. However, God had a different plan.

On Halloween night, that same year, I continued to hear the Lord speaking to my heart about writing this book. When I awoke the next morning, the first thought in my head was "You need to write this book about people living through troubled times." I knew it was time to be obedient and listen to God. While I was still in bed, I closed my eyes and prayed this simple prayer:

> *"Dear God…If you want me to write this book, then you will need to tell me what to write. I have no clue."*

I then grabbed my phone and opened the "notes app." For the next two hours, I experienced the most amazing download from heaven. God provided the name of the book along with a list of chapter titles and the people that I should interview. I then wrote the introduction and conclusion to the book. The words just flowed from my head to my fingers onto the phone. It was incredible.

Over the next few months, out of faith, I began to reach out to the people that God asked me to interview. I openly discussed my book journey, talked about the book's title, and then shared that God had given me their name to contact regarding a specific chapter in the book. I was shocked to discover how quickly people agreed to be interviewed and were anxious to share their story. And so, the journey began.

Throughout this process, I learned and re-learned that:

- God prepared me, through the painful times in my life, to write this book.

- Everyone wants to be loved and accepted. The good news, Jesus loves and accepts us where we are in our lives, the way we are, no matter what we have done. He hears our prayers.

- Many, many people are experiencing trials and heartbreaks in their lives. We need to take time, be present, and be aware of people around us that need our compassion and support.

- God has given every person "free will." Sometimes "free will" results in bad things happening to good people.

- Setting aside time to pray and listen to Our Heavenly Father's guidance and direction must be a daily priority, not an afterthought.

- God places people in our lives just when we need them.

- All our prayers are heard, but not all prayers are answered.

- God does amazing things when people fully surrender to Him.

- When you ask God for help, you must 100% believe in Him. Don't have doubts about God's power to intervene and help you. Just believe!

- No matter what hardship, sickness, or tragedy you are going through, God is with you! He will not abandon you – He will carry you through your storms if you will simply trust and obey.

- The Bible is amazing. God's word provides free advice, counsel, direction, support, perspective, and hope. Sometimes the Bible verses seem to come alive just when you need them. Bible verses you have read numerous times, suddenly take on new significance and meaning for you.

- We are all blessed and loved by God.

Thank God for the RAINBOW!

CPSIA information can be obtained
at www.ICGtesting.com
Printed in the USA
BVOW11s1826100817
491675BV00006B/16/P